FIFTY PENGUIN YEA

This book has been published to accompany the exhibition
FIFTY PENGUIN YEARS
at the Royal Festival Hall, London, 21 September–27 October 1985.
The exhibition has been made possible
by generous sponsorship from Pearson plc.

EXHIBITION DESIGN *by David Lloyd Jones and Simon Barker*
EXHIBITION TYPOGRAPHY *by Cinamon and Kitzinger*
FLOOR COVERINGS *designed and painted by Simon Barker*
INSTALLATION AND PHOTOGRAPHIC REPRODUCTION *by Replicards Ltd*
PHOTOGRAPHIC ORIGINATION *by Michael Dyer Associates*

The video Penguins in the Making
has been generously sponsored by Richard Clay plc

Published on the occasion of Penguin Books'

fiftieth anniversary

FIFTY PENGUIN YEARS

Penguin Books Ltd, Harmondsworth, Middlesex, England
Viking Penguin Inc., 40 West 23rd Street, New York, New York 10010, USA
Penguin Books Australia Ltd, Ringwood, Victoria, Australia
Penguin Books Canada Ltd, 2801 John Street, Markham, Ontario, Canada L3R 1B4
Penguin Books (N.Z.) Ltd, 182–190 Wairau Road, Auckland 10, New Zealand

First published 1985
Copyright © Penguin Books 1985
All rights reserved

Made and printed in Great Britain by
Balding + Mansell Limited
Wisbech, Cambs, England
Typeset in 9pt Monophoto Photina
Designed by Cinamon and Kitzinger

CONTENTS

Colour plates appear between pages 112 and 113

Malcolm Bradbury

FOREWORD

The words 'Penguin' and 'paperback' are so intimately entwined that from time to time we need to remind ourselves that they are not totally synonymous. When, in May 1935, Allen Lane, then at The Bodley Head, announced his famous first ten titles, 'in strong, paper covers . . . at sixpence per volume', there were already cheap paper-bound books available. What made Penguin different was the basic quality of the titles. The nervous book trade had to be reassured that many of these Penguins had been available in 'cheap editions' for some time and posed no threat. The excellence of a title was guaranteed by Lane's own judgement, and his own selection test: 'That is a book I have always meant to read: I will get it now.' It was the high standard of selection, and the good proportion of major contemporary works that made Penguin quite remarkable, and made many people think of Penguins, not just as a form of publishing commerce, but as the stuff of an entire education.

What Allen Lane had done was to break open the 'cultured circuit', the closed community of already established readers, and, in a 1930s book trade that was growing much more commercial and commodity-oriented, greatly broaden that establishment. Into the world of 'yellowback' publishing, of romance, spies and crime, he brought good books, radically changing habits of book purchase and book ownership.

It was with the advent of the war, however, that Penguins really came into their own. Economically produced and marvellously distributed, they reached, at a time of paper-rationing and reduced book publication, a massive audience newly eager to rediscover the culture they were fighting for. These are the books with the cracking spines, and the advertisements for Pears Jiff Shaving Stick ('to soothe the savage beard') that still sit on my shelves.

One of the great cultural success stories of wartime was *Penguin New Writing*, which married avant-garde writing with a vast and enthusiastic general readership. It was avidly sought, and sales reached 100,000 copies. It is hard to conceive of a literary magazine selling in such numbers today, in spite of a larger population and greater affluence. Lehmann said: 'I believe that *New Writing* could and should appeal to a far wider public than that which a book costing 6s. or 7s. 6d. reaches.' Lane agreed, supporting the venture with his paper supplies. Lehmann also appealed for 'a regular flow of stories, poems and sketches . . . by soldiers, sailors, airmen and others directly involved in the operations of war, and about their own experiences'. In this way, work by many of the most notable writers of the thirties, British and European, from MacNeice to Malraux, Spender to Silone, was soon being reprinted alongside a topical series of articles: 'The Way We Live Now', 'Shaving Through the Blitz', 'Books and the War'. All this helped create a new mood of literary culture in wartime: a mood of common cause, shared experience, and the dissolution of political and cultural barriers.

After the war, the anthology, as Lehmann put it, 'spread its wings into the thundery post-war day'. It sought to reflect new cultural directions, notably with young American writers. It printed Saul Bellow, Lionel Trilling, Tennessee Williams and Eudora Welty. What it seemed not to find was a parallel British movement. Annual subscriptions declined, and one of the sadder moments of the austerity age was its disappearance in 1950.

It left, none the less, a substantial legacy for the future: the proven feasibility of an alliance between serious contemporary writing and a large readership. It provided the soil out of which grew such ventures as the famous Alvarez *New Poetry*, Penguin Modern Poets, and that invaluable relationship now forged between Penguin and perhaps our most important current literary magazine, *Granta*. These developments suggested that a paperback house did not simply reprint, but influenced cultural trends, and that there was an intimate relation between cultural vitality and the activity of the publisher in the paperback market.

By the late 1950s, things were changing for Penguin as the number of paperback houses increased, and the competition for paperback rights intensified. In America, major paperback series like Anchor, Meridian and Compass (the paperback arm of Viking, now part of Penguin) developed lists which became the stuff of the modern intellectual's repertoire. In Britain, new houses seemed to outrun Penguin in the matter of contemporary experimental fiction, and in the new debates raging in politics, psychology and sociology, and Penguin went through a period of appearing staid and dull, encumbered with a heavy and traditional backlist. As the market became more and more competitive, former Penguin authors appeared with new houses and imprints. Some decisions had to be made: in the sixties and early seventies they were. New standards of editing sharpened up some of the classic series, and major projects like the *Pelican Guide to English Literature* were given an update. New titles were added on a massive scale, increasing the list from 2,000 to 5,000 books, till today the huge list of titles in print makes up a vast modern university.

The growth of the paperback trade had led to many dire warnings that it would threaten serious writing. I believe that it was partly through the vigour and purposefulness of Penguin's editorial policy in the postwar years that this did not happen. Paperback publishing is publishing for the mass market, and a good deal of it is entirely derivative, dependent on the books initiated by the hardback publisher. But Penguin, forged in the educational and social ideas of the 1930s and 1940s, initiated a large part of its own lists, and extended its role when the market grew in the 1960s. The gap in publication time between hardback and paperback narrowed, and every author came to expect a paperback sale.

When I was an avid youthful reader, the Penguin book became the basis of my literary education. I read *Penguin New Writing* with

voracity, and celebrated when ten Evelyn Waughs and ten D. H. Lawrences came out together. When I was a student, at the start of the 1950s, there was still a curious impropriety about accumulating a library largely made up of paperbacks, but I was able in this way to build up a collection of personal classics in all the major areas, from the fiction of the past and present, through poetry and drama to philosophy and history. This was, for me, the importance of the paperback revolution: the endless extension of the canon of reading. I came to regard Penguin Books, not as a publishing house, but as a major national institution, like the BBC, and noted whom it honoured, and whom it failed to honour. One recognized the judgements, and (overlooking all such problems such as rights) criticized the omissions.

Why had Penguin never done Erich Auerbach's great book *Mimesis*? When would it discover Borges? (It soon did.) When will it do Peter Handke's fiction? In short, publication in Penguin meant that a book was available for discussion, and, if you were, like me, an academic, for student purchase and teaching. One of my own most pleasurable moments was passing beyond being a reader, and entering the lists as a writer. When my first novel, *Eating People is Wrong*, appeared in Penguin in 1962, I regarded it as a step towards canonization.

So, fifty years on, Penguin has a double look to it: that of an old and respected British institution, and that of an innovative and challenging international publishing house, obviously invigorated by its American connections. Ever since André Maurois appeared in the first ten, and John Lehmann made the case for including the European dimension of contemporary writing, the international flavour of Penguins has always been strong. The merger with Viking in America has enlarged this, bringing in some excellent new series like the Viking Portables, and the classics from Viking Penguin, and, I hope, a recognition that, however much the British may be tempted into provinciality, they possess a world language and a literary and intellectual life that functions on a global scale. Fiction is my strongest interest, and in my view we have seen a major new international movement in the novel since the early 1970s, in which British writers and readers play their part.

Fifty years ago, it would have been strange to think of throwaway paperbacks as part of anything that could seriously be called culture, but a great deal has happened since then. Upstairs in my own house, my younger son is busy Penguin-collecting: the first 1,000 titles, and the green-and-white-banded detective series, up to the apocalyptic moment when they began to have illustrated covers. Watching the volumes spread through the house, it seems to me fairly clear that Penguin has a lot to celebrate.

July 1985

Linda Lloyd Jones

FIFTY YEARS OF PENGUIN BOOKS

1935-7

'The Penguins are Coming'*

Allen Lane was sixteen years old when he left his home town of Bristol in 1919 to join his uncle's publishing firm, John Lane The Bodley Head, in Vigo Street, London. In the 1890s the company was renowned for publishing the infamous Oscar Wilde and the avant-garde literary periodical the *Yellow Book*, with its audacious illustrations by Aubrey Beardsley. John Lane recognized, however, that the effects of the First World War had deprived the firm of much of its vigour and was determined that someone young, preferably a member of his family, should be trained to take over the running of the company. John Lane had no children of his own but often visited his relatives in the West Country. He proposed to his cousin, Mrs Williams, that he should take her son Allen into the firm if he would change his surname from Williams to Lane. As he had been christened Allen Lane Williams there was little problem, but for the sake of consistency the whole family altered their name by deed poll to Williams-Lane.

By 1934, nearly ten years after John Lane's death, it was clear to Allen Lane, by then Managing Director of the firm, that The Bodley Head was in financial trouble, and dramatic action was needed to rescue the company from eventual collapse. In September of that year he attended a weekend conference convened by bookseller Basil Blackwell and publisher Stanley Unwin: the theme was 'The New Reading Public'. The fifty delegates un-animously concluded that a new reading public certainly existed, but that only Wool-worth's and the tuppenny libraries were cater-ing for it. They failed, however, to agree upon how best publishers and booksellers could provide for this new market.

Perhaps the two problems – how to make The Bodley Head financially secure and how to provide books for the new reading public –

*Publishers' Circular, 25 May 1935.

The young Allen Lane in about 1929.

resolved themselves in Allen Lane's mind when, after a weekend with Agatha Christie and her husband, he searched Exeter railway station's bookstall for something to read on the journey back to London. Finding only popular magazines and reprints of Victorian novels, he was finally convinced of the real need for cheap editions of good-quality contemporary writ-ing. By the end of the month he had started approaching London publishers for the rights to reprint their leading authors' works in a new series of books to sell at the price of ten cigarettes: sixpence each.

The book trade viewed his scheme with great suspicion, fearing it would undermine the market for hardback fiction, selling at seven or eight shillings and sixpence, and

13

(Left) *The Bodley Head premises, 8 Vigo Street, London, in about 1895.
Drawing by Edmund H. New.*

(Below, left) *Probably the best known early cheap reading matter is the Victorian 'penny dreadful'.*

(Below) *The 'sixpenny' was not a new concept. But 6d. in 1935 was better value than in 1903.*

(Opposite page, left) *Benn's Sixpenny Library of the 1920s and 1930s was a collection of miniature non-fiction texts.*

(Opposite page, right) *In childhood Allen Lane read the paper-covered Stead's Books for the Bairns. Gulliver's Travels was heavily edited for the series.*

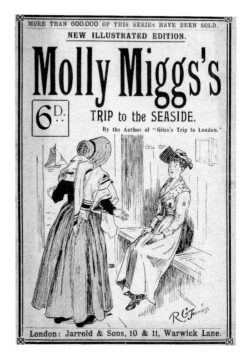

annihilate what they deemed their 'cheap editions', small hardbacks retailing at two or three shillings and sixpence (five to seven times more expensive than the price Allen Lane had in mind). His critics were also quick to point out that similar ventures had been tried since the end of the century and most had failed miserably – including The Bodley Head's own ill-fated ninepenny series which is reputed to have lost the company the vast sum of £9,000 between 1932 and 1933.

Harold Raymond, Managing Director of Chatto and Windus, wrote to Allen Lane in November 1934 declining to have any part in the new series, saying:

The steady cheapening of books is in my opinion a great danger in the trade at present, and I sometimes think booksellers have to be saved from themselves in this respect. It is they who have so constantly clamoured for us publishers to 'meet depression with depression prices'. Yet it is this lowering of prices which is one of the chief reasons why our trade is finding it so hard to recover from the slump. (Letter from Harold Raymond to Allen Lane, 1 November 1934)

Allen Lane's co-directors at The Bodley Head were also convinced that the sixpenny series was a rash enterprise, and accordingly refused to finance the venture, agreeing only to distribute the books under the firm's name.

Jonathan Cape was the first publisher Allen Lane managed to persuade to part with titles for his dubious project. He later recalled:

Jonathan Cape [had] the list of the nineteen-twenties: Hemingway, Sinclair Lewis, Beverley Nichols, Mary Webb. I went to see Jonathan, and said, 'I want ten to start and ten to follow, and I want ten of them from yours.' I told him which. I was offering then twenty-five pounds advance on account of a royalty of a farthing a copy, payable on publication. He wrote back after a while, saying, 'You can have them for an advance of forty pounds each, all payable on signature, on account of a royalty of three-eighths of a penny.' So I got them.

Years later, when the trade was not very good, I was talking to Jonathan and he said, 'You're the b— that has ruined this trade with your ruddy Penguins.' I replied, 'Well, I wouldn't have got off to such a good start if you hadn't helped me.' He

BENN'S SIXPENNY
LIBRARY, No. 252
★
OLIVER
CROMWELL
By HILAIRE BELLOC

LONDON: ERNEST BENN LIMITED

8   GULLIVER'S TRAVELS IN LILIPUT.

pull, which gave me excessive pain, I a little loosened the strings that tied down my hair on the left side, so that I was just able to turn my head about two inches. But the creatures ran off a second time, before I could seize them; whereupon there was a great shout in a very shrill accent, and after it ceased I heard one of them cry aloud, Tolgo Phonac; when in an instant I felt above a hundred arrows discharged on my left hand, which pricked me like so many needles; and besides they shot another flight into the air, as we do bombs in Europe, whereof many, I suppose, fell on my body (though I felt them not) and some on my face, which I immediately covered with my left hand. When this shower of arrows was over I fell a-groaning with grief and pain, and then, striving again to get loose, they discharged another volley larger than the first, and some

TAUCHNITZ EDITION

COLLECTION OF BRITISH AND AMERICAN AUTHORS

VOL. 4920

THE GOOD COMPANIONS

BY

J. B. PRIESTLEY

In Two Volumes. — Vol. 2

LEIPZIG: BERNHARD TAUCHNITZ

PARIS: LIBRAIRIE GAULON & FILS, 39, RUE MADAME

Not to be introduced into the British Empire and U.S.A.

(Above) *Tauchnitz editions were perhaps the genuine precursors of today's paperbacks. Begun in Leipzig in 1842, the series was not for sale in Britain, its Empire or America.*

(Below) *Allen Lane wanted a 'dignified but flippant' name for his new series, suggesting an animal or bird. His secretary, Joan Coles, came up with the idea of a Penguin. Edward Young of the Production Department went off to London Zoo to sketch the new symbol.*

said, 'I know damn well you wouldn't, but like everybody else in the trade I thought you were bound to go bust, and I thought I'd take four hundred quid off you before you did.' (Michael S. Howard: *Jonathan Cape, Publisher*, Jonathan Cape, London, 1971)

Allen Lane was forced to undertake the Penguin series as a private enterprise, so he enrolled the support of his younger brothers, Richard and John, who by that time were also working for The Bodley Head. They estimated that to break even they would need to sell 17,000 copies of each title, five or six times the number usually sold of a new hardback book. John Lane, who had just returned from a world tour as a representative for several London publishing houses, wrote to all his newly made contacts overseas; Dick Lane visited bookshops in and around London; and Allen Lane toured the rest of Britain. Booksellers everywhere were deeply sceptical, complaining that they would never sell enough copies to make it worth their while to stock them, and, of course, that the paper covers would be damaged within hours of being on the shelf. Just before publication day, 30 July 1935, only 7,000 copies of each title had been ordered.

The series was aimed at 'the new reading public' but Allen Lane found that these readers *have not reached the state of self-confidence in which they can feel at home in a bookshop . . . The great majority of the public, which must include many potential book buyers, are scared of walking through our doors. Their fears are twofold: firstly of their financial liability – our windows mostly stocked with 12s. 6d. to 18s. biographies and*

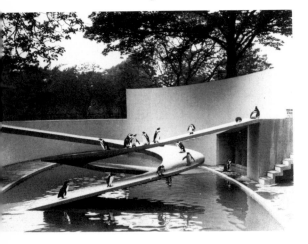

7s. 6d. novels foster this; secondly, of displaying their ignorance. They feel at home in a tuppenny library or at Woolworth's, where they get the same amount of attention if they spend 5s. or if they go out with nothing at all; but the idea of braving an empty bookshop with two or three assistants lying in wait behind the shelves is too much for them. (Bookseller, 22 May 1935)

And so Allen Lane promptly went off to see Clifford Prescott, the chief haberdashery buyer at Woolworth's, for whom in 1934 he had produced a sixpenny edition of Walt Disney's *Three Little Pigs*. Although the famous '3d. and 6d. store' had sold over 130,000 copies of this illustrated book in under a year, Prescott was doubtful about contemporary fiction, bound in paper covers and without even a pictorial jacket. As they discussed the Penguin titles, Mrs Prescott arrived at the office and, when asked by her husband what she thought of the books, declared she had read a number of them and thought them excellent. Prescott was persuaded to take ten sets of the ten titles for twelve branches. Within a week of publication there was much jubilation in The Bodley Head office when Woolworth's placed a consignment order for 63,500 Penguins.

The first ten titles selected were a mixture of biography, detective fiction and novels, all by contemporary writers and bound in bright colours, coded to make each genre easily identifiable: blue for biography, green for crime and detective fiction and orange for novels. The press and public alike showed their immediate approval with enthusiastic reviews and undreamed-of sales.

(Above, right) *In 1934 The Bodley Head published Walt Disney's* Silly Symphonies. Three Little Pigs *sold so well at 2s. 6d. that Allen Lane produced a 6d. edition which proved three times as popular.*

(Right) *'Now prepare for a shock. We have in preparation what promises to cause something of a revolution in English book publishing . . .' ran the text to this advertisement in The Bodley Head's journal, the* Bodleian, *Spring 1935.*

THE PENGUINS ARE COMING

The "Penguin Books," the new paper-bound sixpenny editions of modern literature, will shortly be on the bookstalls in their gaily coloured jackets. (See page 4.) Here are the first ten titles to be published simultaneously on June 28th :—

1 ARIEL by André Maurois
2 FAREWELL TO ARMS by Ernest Hemingway
3 POET'S PUB by Eric Linklater
4 MADAME CLAIRE by Susan Ertz
5 THE BELLONA CLUB by Dorothy L. Sayers
6 THE MYSTERIOUS AFFAIR AT STYLES by Agatha Christie
7 TWENTY-FIVE by Beverley Nichols
8 WILLIAM by E. H. Young
9 GONE TO EARTH by Mary Webb
10 CARNIVAL by Compton Mackenzie

SIXPENCE EACH

(Above) *The Bodley Head took the front page of the* Bookseller *on 3 July 1935 to reassure customers that, despite Penguins, they were still 'The Same Old Firm'.*

---

3 *The Grove*
Highgate Village
N.6
Telephone Mountview 6603

22nd July, 1935.

Dear Lane,

These Penguin books are amazingly good value for money. If you can make the series pay for itself - with such books at such price - you will have performed a great publishing feat.

Yours sincerely,

Allen Lane, Esq.,
Vigo Street, W.1.

SIXPENNY NOVELS:
A PUBLISHING TRIUMPH
declared a half-inch tall headline in the *Sunday Referee* on 28 July 1935.
The courage behind it is as admirable as the volumes. Neatly bound, well printed and perfectly pocketable, these volumes are marvels of mass production
commented the *Daily Herald* on 1 August 1935.
Penguin Books at sixpence apiece . . . have the virtue of bringing books of a wide variety within as easy range as a seat at 'the talkies' or a pint of ale
expounded the *Manchester Guardian* on 1 August 1935.
Just five months later, on 24 January 1936, the *Star* announced:
A MILLION SALE. In spite of some opposition, one of the biggest publishing successes of last year was The Bodley Head's sixpenny series of Penguin Books.
But the overnight success of Penguin came too late to save The Bodley Head from going into liquidation. To stop his profitable series falling prey to the 'old firm's' creditors, Allen Lane quickly raised the £100 nominal capital necessary to form a limited company, and on 15 January 1936 Penguin Books received its Certificate of Incorporation.
For the first hectic eighteen months, business was conducted from a former Bodley Head store in the crypt of Holy Trinity Church, Marylebone Road. It became the warehouse, accounts department and distribution centre for ten million books. Arriving from the printers by van, packed in parcels of a hundred, they were quickly trundled to the side of the church where a grille in the paving had been removed to expose a fairground slide, installed as the easiest means of receiving the books at speed. Conditions in the crypt were far from salubrious: thousands of books were piled on benches in front of vaults carrying inscriptions to departed Victorians; noise had to be kept to a minimum when services were

(Left) *Letters of congratulation arrived from reviewers, readers and authors, including J. B. Priestley. But he had to wait another thirteen years to become a Penguin author.*

being held in the church above; the lavatory consisted of a bucket in the corner; and

the mice . . . used to give us a bit of a fright in the middle of the night when you were writing invoices . . . Rapley [later to become the London representative] used to cross himself like mad. (Richard Lane quoted in *A Report on Penguin World*, compiled by Mass-Observation (unpublished), 1947)

For a weekly wage of 37s. 6d. – plus a penny a day for the public lavatories across the road at Great Portland Street underground station – a dozen dedicated staff worked from 8 am to 6 pm on weekdays and to 1 pm on Saturdays.

(Left) *Holy Trinity Church: A fairground slide was the quickest method of receiving deliveries from the printers into the crowded crypt. Parcels of Penguins were despatched from the crypt by horse-drawn wagon.*

(Below) *A cutting from the* Bookseller, *30 January 1936. Determined to keep Penguins at sixpence, Allen Lane had to print at least 50,000 copies and sell over 700 a week. The moment sales fell short of this the title was dropped. Juggling print quantity with price is a feature common to 1935 and 1985.*

PENGUIN BOOKS

SOME TITLES DROPPED

Mr. Allen Lane writes to *The Bookseller* as follows :—

" As part of our policy in connection with the above series, we intend to drop certain titles from time to time, although they may be on the active list. We feel that by doing this we are furthering the interests of the trade, who will be able to sell other existing editions of the works on the strength of the publicity gained for the titles in question through their inclusion in our series.

" I should be glad, therefore, if I could notify the trade through your columns that from the end of next week the following titles will be answered out of print by us :

No. 4. *Madame Claire*, by Susan Ertz.
No. 6. *The Mysterious Affair at Styles*, by Agatha Christie.
No. 7. *Twenty-Five*, by Beverley Nichols.
No. 8. *William*, by E. H. Young.
No. 9. *Gone to Earth*, by Mary Webb.
No. 10. *Carnival*."

The Penguin van.

DO YOU KNOW THAT

PENGUINS

have sold the absolutely amazing number, in twelve months, of

3,000,000

Such a figure is difficult to grasp. But think this over :—If all that have been sold to date were piled on top of one another, they would reach five times as high as Everest. Placed end to end they would reach from London to Cologne. And taking the average rate of sale, a Penguin Book is sold every ten seconds, day and night, every day of the week, including Sunday.

PEOPLE WANT PENGUINS : IS YOUR STOCK UP-TO-DATE?

Ten new titles published last week.		Outstanding Travel books coming November 12.	
51 MORNING TIDE	Neil Gunn	66 A SURGEON'S LOG	J. Johnson Abrahams
52 THE SPANISH FARM	R. H. Mottram	67 MY SOUTH SEA ISLAND	Eric Muspratt
53 DUSTY ANSWER	Rosamond Lehmann	68 WITH MYSTICS & MAGICIANS IN TIBET	A. David-Neel
54 I AM JONATHAN SCRIVENER	Claude Houghton	69 SOME EXPERIENCES OF A NEW	
55 THE PARTY DRESS	Joseph Hergesheimer	& GUINEA RESIDENT MAGISTRATE :	
56 THE HOUNDS OF SPRING	Sylvia Thompson	70 Vols. 1 & 2. C. A. W. Monckton	
57 THE BLACK DIAMOND	Francis Brett Young		
58 THE POISONED CHOCOLATES CASE	Anthony Berkeley		
59 THREE WIVES	Beatrice Kean Seymour	SIXPENCE EACH	
60 THE DARK INVADER	Captain von Rintelen		

PENGUIN BOOKS LTD., BURY ST., LONDON, W.C.

Weekly Trade Guide, 5 October 1936.

But to keep abreast of the orders, it was not uncommon to work throughout the night, or to see the Managing Director, Allen Lane, and his brothers helping to unload the printers' vans, while packers heaved customers' orders on to the coffin lift at the rear of the building for collection by railway, shipping and delivery agents' lorries. Penguin's own van was driven by Bill Rapley who, wearing a cap, would act as delivery boy, unloading customers' consignments at the back of a shop, and then, exchanging the cap for a trilby, transform himself into the London representative, enter the shop through the front door, meet the bookseller, discuss forthcoming Penguins and take the next week's orders.

On Penguin's first birthday, Allen Lane announced sales of over three million books and a turnover for the book trade of £75,000. The year's bestselling titles had been: Dorothy L. Sayers's *The Unpleasantness at the Bellona Club*, Margot Asquith's *Autobiography*, Beverley Nichols's *Twenty-Five*, Liam O'Flaherty's *The Informer* and Mary Webb's *Gone to Earth*.

To celebrate, Allen Lane bought himself a nine-ton cutter, which he appropriately named *Penguin* (fitting her out with items being sold from the royal yacht *Britannia*), and gave the entire staff of nearly twenty people a day trip by boat-train to Boulogne, Le Touquet and Paris Plage.

1937–9

'The peculiarity of Penguin is that it has put selling into bookselling.'*

When a local authority official condemned working conditions in the crypt, Allen Lane was presented with the opportunity of amalgamating the staff working there with the office staff operating over a motor-car showroom in Great Portland Street. He selected a 3½-acre site at Harmondsworth, fifteen miles west of London, and built a single-storey office with a warehouse at the rear. The land, which today is dominated by the world's busiest airport, Heathrow, was devoted to market gardening in the 1930s, and as the farmer disposing of his fields insisted on an additional payment for the crop of cabbages, so Allen Lane felt compelled to recoup the outlay by selling the vegetables as they matured. On moving to Harmondsworth, Penguin staff found that the walls and roof of the warehouse had been erected, but that only part of the floor had been laid, so they had to pack and despatch 140,000 books a week while picking their way around the cabbages, until the crop was ready for market and the building could be completed.

Friends and colleagues expressed amazement that Allen Lane should expect his business to survive at such a distance from London, but he was convinced that on one site, and without the divisions created by a multi-storey building, the spirit of adventure would be maintained. Although he continued to meet editorial advisers in London, it was not until the late 1950s that additional London offices were leased.

All his employees were aware of the stir Penguins were causing, even if it was difficult for them to believe the claims being made by the press:

WISDOM AT SIXPENCE. The simple evidence of one's eyes, here, there, and everywhere, is enough

*Shelf Appeal, August 1937.

Allen Williams-Lane Sr laid the foundation stone of the new offices on 13 August 1937.

The new headquarters, Bath Road, Harmondsworth. (Topham Picture Library.)

The Lane brothers, Dick, Allen and John, in about 1938.

By spring 1936 Penguin's success had persuaded other publishers to imitate both the format and the ornithological logo.

to show the emergence of a new social habit on a large scale. (*The Times*, 28 September 1937)

Publishers, booksellers, authors and literary critics, on the other hand, hotly disputed the merits of Penguin Books and their fast-appearing imitators. George Orwell, reviewing the third batch of Penguins, complained:

The Penguin Books are splendid value for sixpence, so splendid that if the other publishers had any sense they would combine against them and suppress them. It is, of course, a great mistake to imagine that cheap books are good for the book trade. Actually it is just the other way about. If you have, for instance, five shillings to spend and the normal price of a book is half-a-crown, you are quite likely to spend your whole five shillings on two books. But if books are sixpence each you are not going to buy ten of them, because you don't want as many as ten; your saturation-point will have been reached long before that. Probably you will buy three sixpenny books and spend the rest of your five shillings on seats at the 'movies'. Hence the cheaper books become, the less money is spent on books. This is an advantage from the reader's point of view and doesn't hurt the trade as a whole, but for the publisher, the compositor, the author and the bookseller it is a disaster. (George Orwell, *New English Weekly*, 5 March 1936)

Stanley Unwin, the doyen of publishers, declared:

As Ruskin pointed out, there are dangers in the very cheapness of literature and 'no book is worth anything which is not worth much.' There is already a tendency in the average Englishman's mind to regard any expenditure on books as an extravagance, and it would be sad if the public felt that it had done its share in supporting literature by merely buying a few sixpenny books. (*The Times Literary Supplement*, 19 November 1938)

But Margaret Cole, author, and prominent member of the Fabian Society, counter-attacked:

... it is high time that book-owning should cease to be the preserve of a small class ... it can only be brought to the others by giving them the best you possibly can. (*The Times Literary Supplement*, 26 November 1938)

The Economist supported her argument:

To bring serious books, well printed books and genuine literature to homes where cheap ephemeral trash has been the staple diet is a notable step ... The Penguins and Pelicans succeeded, where decades of sixpennies had failed, for several reasons: they are better produced (costing twopence each to produce against a gross profit of the same sum), and of better quality; they are more recently written works than earlier cheap reprints; and, very important, they are distributed with splendid efficiency and economy through all sorts of outlets all over the world. (The Economist, 3 December 1938)

While arguments raged, Allen Lane was steadily increasing sales through bookshops, railway bookstalls, newsagents, tobacconists, department and chain stores, and even slot machines. Having successfully identified his new reading public, he launched a promotional campaign that was to become legendary. With the exception of Collins, most publishers' advertising was restricted to notices in the trade press and Sunday newspapers. Allen Lane, however, started notifying

(Below) *Allen Lane takes a Penguin from the Penguincubator. It was placed outside Collet's bookshop, Charing Cross Road, London, in July 1937.*

PENGUINCUBATOR

Allen Lane extracts the first book from the automatic machine outside Collet's bookshop. You press sixpence in the slot, punch the key bearing the number you want, lift the slot cover, and there's your book. Ingenious people found, however, that by skilful manipulation of the keys you could get quite a few books for your sixpence. Further experiment, Lane hopes, will make the machine knaveproof.

LONDON FILMS present an ALEXANDER KORDA production.

MERLE **OBERON**

LAURENCE **OLIVIER**

The **DIVORCE OF LADY X**

with BINNIE BARNES RALPH RICHARDSON MORTON SELTEN Photographed in TECHNICOLOR Directed by TIM WHELAN

Programmes begin at 10.0 : 12.15 : 2.30 : 4.35 : 6.50 and 9.15. Sundays at 6.0 & 8.30. "The Divorce of Lady X." showing weekdays at 10.40 : 12.55 : 3.0 : 5.15 : 7.40 : 9.35.

UNITED ARTISTS

Cert 'A'

ODEON *Theatre* LEICESTER SQUARE

(Above) *In January 1938 glamorous Merle Oberon was pictured with a Penguin in the advertisement for the film* The Divorce of Lady X.

booksellers of advertising plans for new titles and issuing gay showcards for display shortly before each publication date. The first time this method was tried, advance orders of 133,000 were immediately obtained. Supplying a list of new titles for shop windows also quickly generated a loyal reading public which expectantly awaited each successive batch.

The chief method of advertising, however, was by direct mail. In the first experiment a business reply card was placed in each book, inviting readers to register their names for receipt of future stocklists, and requesting suggestions for new titles. Within three months Penguin had to pay the Post Office for 26,000 cards, which amounted to a good mailing list – and a bill of £108. The next card inserted required the reader to pay his own postage. By August 1937, 60,000 people were on the mailing list.

For the first two years, Allen Lane managed to keep to the tight profit margins required by a sixpenny series, spending on each book 1.7d. for the dustcover paper, cover board, binding, and printing, and 0.74d. for the text paper. Twopence went to the retailer, and 0.36d. went to the original publisher and author. Allen Lane retained the last 1.20d. to plough back into the company. By the end of 1937,

however, the cost of paper had risen from £14 to £21 per ton, raising the production cost for each book by 0.323d. and substantially cutting the profit margin. Reluctant to reduce the quality of paper or increase the selling price, Allen Lane decided to exploit the advertising possibilities of the books. Penguins had already been carrying leaflets advertising firms such as Air France, KLM Airlines and the Regent Institute, producing a revenue of ten shillings per thousand, so in August 1937 he announced that advertising in black and white would appear on four pages, and possibly also on the back cover in two colours, at a charge of five shillings per thousand. In its first year this advertising generated an income of £2,326 0s. 1d. and rose to a peak in 1944 of £19,039 2s. 4d.

Despite all the voluble opposition from the book trade, a number of publishers were quick to recognize Penguin's potential. Harold

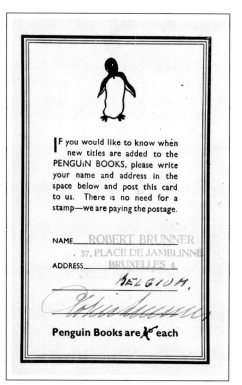

(Above) *This business reply card took thirty-one years to reach Penguin. At least the sender knew in 1968 that the books no longer cost 6d., and had the courtesy to pay the postage.*

(Above) *Additional income was generated for the firm by advertisements on the back cover and end pages of the books.*

Raymond of Chatto and Windus, who had refused to lease reprint rights when approached the year before the series appeared, began to reconsider his position less than two months after the publication of the first ten titles. On 4 October 1935 he wrote to Allen Lane:

The other Partners and I have had a long discussion over your Sixpennies and though our general feeling still is that the book trade as a whole may come to rue the day of the advent of this particular line of publication, the point is that we are quite willing to approach some of our authors and invite them to join in your venture ... although I shall not beg them to accept, I shall certainly not do the reverse.

Raymond proceeded to contact his authors and, true to his word, presented Penguin's terms of £100 advance on a royalty of 30s. per thousand copies sold, prefacing the details with his opinion:

Personally, I must admit that I would not shed tears on their grave, for I doubt if, in the long run, they are going to prove a blessing to impoverished authors, publishers and booksellers. (Letter from Harold Raymond to A. A. Milne, 18 November 1936)

Despite such mistrust, many authors leapt at the opportunity for their works to be produced and distributed by the hundred thousand. At a time when a 7s. 6d. hardback novel was considered a success if it sold 2,000 copies, Allen Lane maintained that a 'comparatively successful' Penguin would sell 150,000 copies, a 'good' Penguin 250,000 and a 'bestseller' 350,000.

The scale of success for the first year's titles – which were not only unabridged, contemporary fiction, but included two volumes of Margot Asquith's *Autobiography*, Alexandra David-Neel's *With Mystics and Magicians in Tibet* and C. A. W. Monckton's *Some Experiences of a New Guinea Resident Magistrate* – inspired one reviewer in the *New English Weekly* to speculate: 'It might be worth experimenting with a sixpenny Rivers or Freud.' Although he cautiously qualified his suggestion with:

There are two obvious objections to this. It might not pay the publisher. It might also be open to criticism from those who feel that vulgarization is not a good thing. (*New English Weekly*, 11 February 1937)

(Above) *'Shakespeare for sixpence, Hamlet for the price of ten Goldflake ... It is the best cheap Shakespeare, and it is pleasant to think of it on stalls at King's Cross and Paddington, with Dashiell Hammett and Edgar Wallace and Dorothy L. Sayers'* (Geoffrey Grigson, Morning Post, 27 April 1937).

But Allen Lane was already way ahead of the reviewer. Late in 1936, while waiting to discuss Penguin sales with the manager of the bookstall at St Pancras Station, he overheard a woman asking:

'Have you got any Pelican Books?' I knew there wasn't such a series – she really meant Penguins. But I knew if somebody else started the word Pelican they'd be stealing some of my thunder. (Interview of Allen Lane by Heather Mansell, 1968, unpublished)

He immediately consulted his lawyer about safeguarding the name Pelican, but was informed that to use it was the only certain method of protection. He then presented the problem to his literary advisers, V. K. Krishna

(Above) *After independence, Pelican advisory editor V. K. Krishna Menon became a cabinet minister in the Indian Government.*

(Below) *William Emrys Williams's association with Pelicans earned him the nickname 'Pelican Bill'. He is pictured with Eunice Frost, who was not only fiction editor for twenty-eight years, but a key figure in Penguin's astounding pre-war and wartime publishing programme.*

Menon, H. L. Beales, William Emrys Williams and Sir Peter Chalmers-Mitchell.

This group of consultant editors made perhaps one of the boldest, most influential policy decisions in British publishing history: they advocated a parallel series concentrating on 'serious' books, breaking the convention of reprinting works already published by other houses, and publishing specially commissioned titles straight into paperback on subjects of interest to 'the intelligent layman'.

The term may sound paternalistic today, but it was used then without condescension by intellectuals committed to education and an equality of opportunity for the working classes. Allen Lane's advisers all held reforming views to different degrees and shared a passionate belief in a mass market for such titles as *Practical Economics* by the Oxford economist G. D. H. Cole, *The Inequality of Man* by J. B. S. Haldane, *The Mysterious Universe* by Sir James Jeans and *Psychopathology of Everyday Life* by Sigmund Freud. By creating Pelicans, they presented the English-speaking world with seminal works on contemporary issues at a price everyone could afford, and secured for Penguin the reputation of a publishing house of stature.

Reviewing the first ten Pelican titles in the *Daily Worker*, R. W. Fletcher expressed the view:

A comparison between the recent arrival of the really cheap book and the discovery of printing may sound far-fetched, but it is perfectly possible that in fifty or a hundred years it will seem a commonplace ... Slowly the best of modern literature will be coming into the hands of any man who wants it, and in the process man himself is going to be changed. (*Daily Worker*, 9 June 1937)

Allen Lane was astute enough, however, to know that even a revolutionary series would need substantial publicity to ensure its success. He achieved this by inviting Bernard Shaw to be Pelican's first author. *The Intelligent Woman's Guide to Socialism and Capitalism*, brought up to date with two additional chapters on Sovietism and Fascism, resulted in an avalanche of publicity for the new series. From this point on there was no stopping new Penguin and Pelican titles, and more sales. In the first year sixty-five books had been published; from August 1936 until the outbreak

(Above) Practical Economics (1937) *was written by G. D. H. Cole specially for the new Pelican imprint, beginning Penguin's tradition of 'original' publishing.*

The Intelligent Woman's Guide *secured enormous press coverage. These headlines appeared in the* Tribune, *18 June 1937 (below), and the* News Chronicle, *21 May 1937 (right).*

(Below) *Bernard Shaw wrote to his printer, Maxwell, on 20 October 1936: 'Prepare for a shock. The Penguin Press wants* The Intelligent Woman's Guide. *A sixpenny edition would be the salvation of mankind' (Line drawing by Joss for* Penguin's Progress, Summer 1939*).*

Shaw "First Edition" at 6d. a Copy

News Chronicle Special

ONE of the inevitable George Bernard Shaw postcards has resulted in the forthcoming publication of what is virtually a first edition of Shaw—in two volumes at 6d. each.

The new edition is "The Intelligent Woman's Guide to Socialism and Capitalism" with the addition of two new chapters on Sovietism and Fascism. a new author's note under the comprehe─ "The Intelligent Woman's Guide" ─alism, Sovietism and Fascism "

Containing 70,000 ─ts, the two volumes a─ ─lican series, th─ ─,000 ─tri-

─rs

Books of The Week
SHAW FOR A SHILLING

Reviewed by J. F. HORRABIN

The Intelligent Woman's Guide to Socialism, Capitalism, Sovietism and Fascism.
By Bernard Shaw. (Pelican Books, 2
vols., 6d. each.)

ALL his life Shaw has " guyed " the Englishman. But in this book, first published nine years ago—when he was over 70—he has written a magnificently English book; perhaps the best all-round statement of that queer medley of ethical idealism and sober matter-of-factness, English Socialism.

He repudiates Class War and Class Struggle—" these terms are misleading imply that all the prole-

to lead to a really effectual suppression of Capitalism.

In short. Mr. Shaw—like so many " practical " Englishmen—is dead sure that a particular job has got to be done, but isn't at all clear *how*. What he is clear about—and that, after all, is enough for one book (more especially if by Shaw) —is that Capitalism is rotten, and the present order of society staggering to its doom.

Two New Chapters

Readers already familiar with The Intelligent Woman's Guide will turn
straight to the two new chapters, on
Sovietism and Fascism, specially written
for this edition.

─armer, Shaw has not a great say; and his

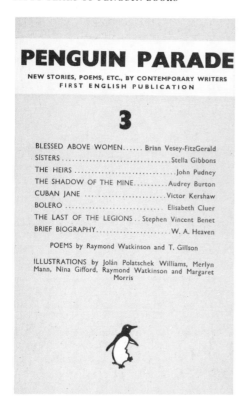

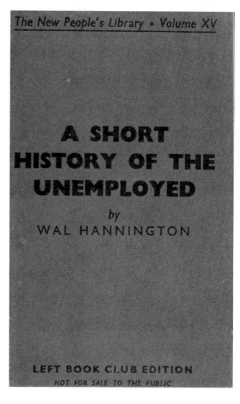

(Above, left) Penguin Parade, *a quarterly anthology of stories, poems and drawings by known and unknown writers and artists. Fourteen issues appeared between 1937 and 1948.*

(Above, right) *Victor Gollancz's Left Book Club was perhaps Penguin's nearest rival, but was considered by some to be 'definitely propagandist, devoted to giving 50,000 readers every month, at a cost of 2s. 6d., a book of fact or theory on the most serious and fundamental problems of the day' (Spectator, 22 July 1938).*

of war in September 1939 another 285 titles appeared, and a total of over twenty-eight and a half million books had been sold.

Probably the greatest proportion of this phenomenal sale is attributable to Penguin Specials, topical books dealing with urgent aspects of world economics and politics. The first of them appeared in November 1937, when Hitler's intentions towards Austria and Czechoslovakia were apparent. Edgar Mowrer's *Germany Puts the Clock Back* was a reprint of the 1933 hardback edition, with a further chapter specially written for Penguin to bring up to date his assessment of Hitler's regime. The initial print run of 50,000 copies was exhausted within a week of appearing on sale – an amazing public response, almost unheard of in today's age of television and the colour supplement. In the following February two more Specials were published: *Mussolini's Roman Empire* by G. T. Garratt and *Blackmail or War?* by Geneviève Tabouis, both specially commissioned by Penguin from journalists well known for their grasp of international

A new series of up-to-the-minute topical books—*Penguin Specials*—to be published from time to time outside our normal schedule. Early next year we shall continue the series with two very important, *entirely new* books on current foreign affairs specially written for us by absolutely reliable experts. Further details of these to follow later.

The first *Penguin Special*—GERMANY PUTS THE CLOCK BACK, by Edgar Mowrer—is not a new book but a reprint of a book which made a sensation when it first appeared and which the author has brought up to date with a new chapter on the present European situation. This was the book, it will be remembered, which caused its author's expulsion from Germany when he was Berlin correspondent for the *Chicago Daily News*, because of its frank account of post-war Germany and Hitler's rise to power. "In a brilliant piece of writing it uncovers the secret forces that are dragging Europe into the abyss." It runs to 288 pages, and is similar in size, price and format to other Penguin Books.

6ᴰ

PENGUIN BOOKS LTD

BATH ROAD : HARMONDSWORTH : MIDDLESEX

(Above, left) *Advertisement for the first Penguin Special, in the* Bookseller, *1 December 1937.*

(Above) *The Duchess of Atholl's book 'has been conceived, written, printed and published with a speed that is almost journalistic . . . The actual writing was begun only eleven weeks ago. The maps, in particular, have needed continual revision as the situation changed'* (Liverpool Daily Post, *10 June 1938*).

(Left) *Advertisement for the Pelican Special* Modern German Art, *'the art that Hitler called "degenerate"'* (Challenge, *7 July 1938*).

" MODERN GERMAN *ART* "

Another up-to-the-minute PELICAN SPECIAL, with 32 gravure plates

THE ART THAT HITLER CALLED " DEGENERATE "

Buy your P E N G U I N S from

PETERS BOOKSHOP		75 HAMMERSMITH ROAD, W.14 (Opposite Olympia)
PROGRESSIVE	,,	17 UNION ST., BELFAST
WORKERS	,,	49 FARRINGDON RD., E.C.1
		66 CHARING X RD., W.C.2
COLLET'S	,,	13/15 HANGING DITCH MANCHESTER
		26 CASTLE ARCADE CARDIFF
		1a DUNDAS ST., GLASGOW
PEOPLES	,,	115 LAVENDER HILL
*PHOENIX BOOK CO.,		66 CHANDOS ST., W.C.2

*(Write for special "all-in" offer for those who purchase any 60 Penguins and Pelicans)

politics. A print run of 50,000 for each title was heralded by the *Bookseller* as a record for new books. The gamble was undoubtedly justified when within four weeks *Blackmail or War?* was reported to be selling 4,000 copies a day.

As war with Germany became only a matter of time, so the Specials came thundering on to the bookstalls. *Europe and the Czechs* by Sheila Grant Duff was typeset, proof-read, corrected, printed and bound within ten days; 50,000 copies were packed and distributed throughout the Friday night, and by Monday morning orders for a further 78,000 copies had been received. *The Jewish Problem* by Louis Golding, *What Hitler Wants* by E. O. Lorimer, *I Was Hitler's Prisoner* by Stefan Lorant, *Poland* by W. J. Rose and *Our Food Problem* by F. Le Gros Clark and R. M. Titmuss were intriguingly interspersed with *Modern German Art* by 'Peter Thoene', *Literary Taste* by Arnold Bennett, *Design* by Anthony Bertram and *The Good Soldier Schweik* by Jaroslav Hašek.

Declaration of war in September 1939 inevitably led to speculation on an international scale about censorship, and security, mobilization and rationing. But Penguin was ready with a veritable torrent of Specials on every topic of debate – *The Government Blue Book (On the Outbreak of World War II)*, *The Internment of Aliens* by F. Lafitte, *Why Britain is at War* by Harold Nicolson, *Must the War Spread?* by D. N. Pritt, *The Penguin Political Atlas* by S. C. Johnson, *Organized Labour in the War* by John Price, *The Case for Family Allowances* by Eleanor F. Rathbone – 153 titles appearing between November 1937 and May 1945.

THE FIRST BIG FIVE OF THE WAR

LIGHT ON MOSCOW
by D. N. PRITT, K.C., M.P.

THE CASE FOR FEDERAL UNION
by W. B. CURRY

WHY BRITAIN IS AT WAR
by HAROLD NICOLSON

THE PENGUIN POLITICAL DICTIONARY
by WALTER TYMER

TRAVELS OF A REPUBLICAN RADICAL IN SEARCH OF HOT WATER
by H. G. WELLS

These Specials with the exception of H. G. Wells have been specially written since the outbreak of war

PENGUIN SPECIALS

This advertisement appeared in January 1940.

1939–45

'One of the most significant events of the 1930s –
comparable in its way with the birth of the BBC
in the previous decade – had been the arrival
of the cheap paperback.'*

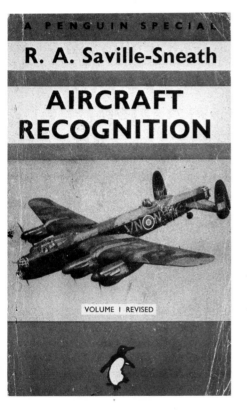

(Above) Aircraft Recognition, *first published in March 1941, was used by civilians and the fighting forces to distinguish enemy planes. For many years it was Penguin's best-selling title.*

*Angus Calder: The People's War, Britain 1939–1945, Jonathan Cape, 1969.

Publishers who had experienced the Great War of 1914–18 predicted that demand for books would surge ahead of the trade's capability to produce them. They were right. In June 1940 the Government introduced paper rationing based on 60 per cent of the amount each firm had used from 1 September 1938 to 31 August 1939. By December 1941 the ration had been reduced to $37\frac{1}{2}$ per cent. Publishers complained bitterly that the year chosen as the basis for rationing was one of the worst ever experienced by the book trade, and prophesied that a book famine would ensue. 'The last thing I want is a best-seller on my hands,' one publisher reported to Alan Moorehead of the *Daily Express*, no doubt anticipating acrimonious correspondence from disappointed customers.

Only Allen Lane was equipped to carry on business with comparative ease: the extraordinary success of Penguin Specials in the months prior to the outbreak of war ensured for Penguin a paper quota larger than almost any other publishing house in Britain. Nevertheless, Penguin's sales of nearly seventeen million books in 1941 dropped to a modest eight and a half million in 1942, when no additional paper could be legally obtained. This, together with a dramatic increase in demand for something to read during the long hours of blackout, forced Penguin to institute its own quota system for bookshops. From January 1942 booksellers were restricted to two-thirds of the quantity of their 1939 orders. Allen Lane had to inform his customers:

To the problem of limitation of paper supplies is now also added that of labour shortage and a certain difficulty in procuring packing materials.

For this reason we regret that we will not be able to supply more than one stock order a month to each customer. (Letter from Allen Lane to booksellers, 31 December 1941)

To soften the blow of his message, he ended the letter:

We are constantly hearing of the existence of rumours that an increase in the price of Penguin, Pelican and Puffin books is contemplated, and I would like to take this opportunity of stating quite definitely that no such move is envisaged. (ibid.)

He must have known, however, that his hand would soon be forced by continually rising paper and production costs; indeed, by the spring of 1942 the price of the by now world-famous 'sixpennies' had escalated to ninepence.

Preoccupation with the lack of paper supplies led to both sensible and fanciful suggestions for economy. The Publishers Association created a committee that met thirteen times within a fortnight to establish a 'Book Production War Economy Agreement' recommending a prescribed typesize, width of margins, and weight for paper and cover boards, all of which were obviously less relevant to Penguin than to other publishers. Home-produced straw was increasingly being used for papermaking instead of esparto grass imported from North Africa, thereby greatly reducing its quality. Denys Kilham Roberts, Secretary of the Society of Authors, even suggested to Allen Lane:

Have you thought of the possibility of publishing in bijou form and tiny print with some sort of magnifying contraption designed to fit the printed page . . . ? (Letter from Denys Kilham Roberts to Allen Lane, 5 June 1941)

(Below) *The publication of* An Outline of European Architecture (1943) *marked the beginning of a remarkable publishing relationship with art historian Nikolaus Pevsner.*

(Below) *Updated, and still in print forty-two years later, the book has been translated into sixteen languages and has sold almost a million copies throughout the world.*

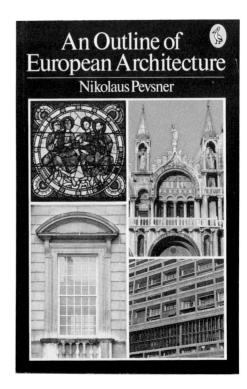

Although Penguin did not adopt this last solution, it did quickly abandon dust jackets, and had to accept books bound with a couple of staples rather than sewn. Authors too were sometimes politely requested to reduce the length of their manuscripts in the interests of economy.

One wartime hazard Penguin did manage to avoid was the destruction of stock by enemy bombing. It is estimated that other publishers lost twenty million books during air raids on London. In the light of this, the inconvenience caused by His Majesty's Government's requisitioning of the Penguin building for aircraft repairs must have seemed a minor price to pay for the relative security of rural Middlesex.

'BOOKS FOR THE TROOPS'
(*Ayrshire Post*, 13 October 1939)

On the declaration of war, local newspapers immediately started printing appeals for the donation of reading matter to the armed forces. Invariably Penguin Books were cited as ideal in size and subject matter, in part, perhaps, because the charitable bodies organizing collections had considerable experience of receiving

unsuitable material . . . church magazines dated 1928 and Christian Heralds of the dim past.
(*Birmingham Post*, 21 November 1939)

This call for books for troops, as well as a salvage drive, initiated by the Ministry of Supply in an endeavour to recycle paper, led to a plea being printed in each Penguin requesting the reader to hand in the book at a local Post Office when he had finished it. In all, fifty-six million volumes (including Penguins) were collected under this scheme, five million of which were sent to the Forces, and one million to replenish bombed library stocks.

The full use of our scientific resources is essential if we are to win the war. To-day they are being half used. This book not only analyses the conditions which have led to this dangerous state of affairs, but also shows where science could be applied with immediate benefit to our national effort. It has been written by 25 scientists, all of whom speak with authority in their own fields.

(Above) *In summer 1940, twenty-five eminent scientists, including Solly Zuckerman and J. D. Bernal, were invited by Allen Lane to express publicly their view that 'A large proportion of scientific brains in the country are not being used at all, and due to defects of organization, most of those that are being used are not working at anything like their possible efficiency.' Within six weeks of the invitation* Science in War *was on sale throughout Britain. The outspoken Special is credited with directly influencing the government appointment of scientists to warfare research.*

(Above) *Paternoster Row, the heartland of British publishing, was badly bombed during the war. Drawing by R. G. Mathews, 1941 (Guildhall Library).*

33

(Above) *Penguins found their way to camps in Italy for soldiers resting from the North African campaigns (Imperial War Museum).*

(Below) *'Handy for haversacks,' declared the* Nottinghamshire Guardian *on 16 November 1939 (Imperial War Museum).*

Allen Lane was immediately aware of the potential new readership presented by the countless men and women on active service overseas, as well as those in remote or inaccessible units, such as searchlight clusters, Ack-Ack batteries or corvette and submarine crews located all around the British Isles. His genuine desire to help the war effort quickly led in the spring of 1940 to the production of Penguins in special Services Edition covers for

distribution through the Services Central Book Depot in London. The speed of his enterprise, and its success, encouraged him in December 1941 to consider publishing a series of books exclusively for the fighting forces. Together with William Emrys Williams, then Director of the Army Bureau of Current Affairs, he convinced the War Office not only of the importance of books in maintaining morale, but of Penguin's receiving an extra allocation of paper to produce them.

The Forces Book Club issued ten titles a month from October 1942 to September 1943, and admirably endeavoured to maintain a balance between modern fiction, crime, travel, world affairs, biography, science, humour, military operations, and post-war reconstruction with such titles as: *Put Out More Flags* (Evelyn Waugh), *Brighton Rock* (Graham Greene), *An Anthology of War Poetry* (ed. Julian Symons), *Murder by Burial* (Stanley Casson), *Growing-Up in New Guinea* (Margaret Mead), *Nazis in Norway* (Ake Fen), *Disraeli* (André Maurois), *Social Life in the Insect World* (J. H. Fabre), *A Cuckoo in the Nest* (Ben Travers), *Guerrilla War in Abyssinia* (W. E. D. Allen) and *Town Planning* (Thomas Sharp). Regrettably, the well-intentioned selections had a limited appeal amongst the Forces, as they were inevitably competing with books

which, if they cannot be classified as outright pornography, would require a micrometer to detect the difference. (Bookseller, February 1942)

These were being published by the scores of 'mushroom' firms springing up almost weekly, producing books on paper from dubious sources.

The Penguin Services Editions continued however, as did the Prisoner of War Book Service whereby, for an annual subscription of three guineas, 120 Penguins would be distributed through organizations such as the Red Cross to prisoner of war camps in Germany and Italy. The titles for this series first had to be vetted by the British censors in case vital information of use to the enemy might inadvertently be contained within the text. Once delivered, they were again scrutinized, this time by the resident German security officer, to ensure that the books' contents would not give prisoners ideas of disobedience or escape. There is no doubt that these Red

Cross parcels, containing also sweets and warm clothing, letters and photographs, were responsible for keeping prisoners alive, both spiritually and physically.

PROLIFERATION OF PENGUINS

The ever-growing demand for books at home and abroad led Stanley Unwin to lament:
. . . for nearly forty years I had prayed for an increased demand for books, and it was indeed ridiculous that it should come at a moment when it was impossible to supply it. (Sir Stanley Unwin: *The Truth About a Publisher*, Allen and Unwin, 1960)

But in spite of the paper shortages Penguin's response was to expand and develop its range of books. During those six years of war, Penguin initiated no less than nineteen new series with over 700 titles – half of which

(Above) *King Penguins were illustrated with sixteen pages in eight-colour offset and had thirty-two pages of text, all for a shilling.*

(Below) *A few Penguins were printed in Egypt in 1942/3, under licence to W. Jeffery Eady, for sale to besieged French expatriates.*

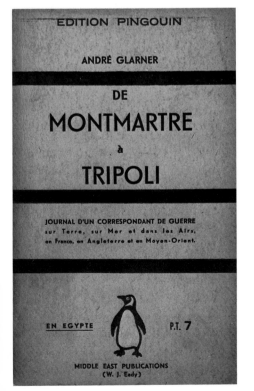

were original works, not reprints – which it achieved with a staff that never exceeded forty people.

King Penguins began the avalanche of new series in November 1939. They had been in preparation since December 1938, and now launched Penguin into the field of colour illustration. Seventy-six of these charming little hardback books with such titles as *Elizabethan Miniatures, Edible Fungi, British Moths, A Book of Scripts* and *Egyptian Paintings* appeared, first under Elizabeth Senior's editorship, and after her death in 1941 until the series ended in 1959, under Nikolaus Pevsner. Sir Roy Strong, Director of the Victoria and Albert Museum, recently recalled:
The King Penguin series, now collectors' items (we've nearly completed our set) but then, in the dark days of the war and its austerity aftermath, one of the only modestly priced art books with colour plates. What a debt one owes. ('Paperbacks, But What a Spine', *The Times*, 16 June 1984)

(Left) 'Dolf Hitler gif a barty . . . (*December 1940*). *Between June 1940 and March 1941 Feliks Topolski produced two humorous and two patriotic prints for sale at 6d. each. To his surprise, in 1944 he found the* Winston Churchill *print for sale in Egypt with 'We shall never surrender . . .' in Arabic. A case of pirating?*

The first of four prints by Topolski, *Winston Churchill: 'We shall never surrender . . .'*, appeared in June 1940. A limited edition of 25,000 was printed by colour lithography and sold at sixpence each in newsagents and bookshops.

The Penguin Hansard was produced in response to the nation's desire to learn precisely what its leaders were saying in the House of Commons. The first volume covered the period 24 August 1939, the last week of peace, to 19 May 1940 and Churchill's famous 'blood and tears' speech. One hundred thousand copies were printed in July, but were suddenly banned from sale by the Treasury. The press speculated that the order may have been imposed for political reasons (as well as those of government monopoly), but a public outcry saved the new series, and it went on to produce a further five digests of verbatim quotations from outstanding speeches.

Penguin New Writing, Penguin's greatest wartime success, was launched in December 1940. Like *Penguin Parade*, it was an anthology of stories, poems and, from volume 13 onwards, illustrations. John Lehmann began editing *New Writing* for The Bodley Head in 1936. It was immediately hailed as 'the most adventurous modern publication' and 'a kind of international clearing house for new writers', but as war approached and The Bodley Head could no longer continue to publish *New Writing* Allen Lane welcomed the opportunity to produce it as a new Penguin series. Forty volumes appeared between December 1940 and September 1950, selling more than 75,000 copies per issue at the

(Left) *Before the days of broadcast excerpts from parliamentary debates, the public had to consult* Hansard, *the official verbatim transcript of each day's proceedings. To help keep the nation informed during the darkest days of the war,* Penguin produced six digests of debates.

height of the war. Undoubtedly the figure would have been higher if more paper had been available, but Allen Lane restricted Lehmann to five tons for each volume – the equivalent to the total annual allocation for another London publisher, the Hogarth Press.

Penguin New Writing, along with Cyril Connolly's *Horizon*, was the flagship of literary culture during the war years. Today it presents us with a catalogue of now famous names – Graham Greene, Alun Lewis, Julian Maclaren-Ross, W. H. Auden, Stephen Spender, Laurie Lee, Roy Fuller, George Barker, George Orwell, Christopher Isherwood, V. S. Pritchett, Elizabeth Bowen and many others, all contributing, as John Lehmann remarked in volume 40, to 'a story, we believe we can say without vainglory, that forms part of the history of our time'. Traditionally anthologies are difficult to sell, but *New Writing* successfully combined the best of contemporary fiction with vivid, often humorous, portrayals of everyday life in blitzed Britain or the front line, and reports on theatre, ballet and cinema. Lehmann endowed the series with the flavour of an arts journal which, for those under siege in Britain or fighting abroad, offered a lifeline to contemporary culture.

Demand for the series declined, however, almost as soon as the war was over, possibly because the country's culture seemed no longer under threat. Readers now had the leisure to get back to full-length novels and the re-emerging magazines, or go to the cinema and theatre.

The exasperating difficulties of publishing in wartime were spelt out for readers by Lehmann in July 1941:

First of all, the authors have to write their contributions; they promise them by a certain day; but in the meantime Fanfarlo's typewriter may have been put out of action by Mrs Greenbaum's land-mine, and Robert Pagan's beautiful hand-written manuscript may have met with Nazi fires on its way through the post, and arrive charred and soggy a week late. Next, the contributions have to be set up in type and proofs corrected; enemy action may cause more delays here, and an Editor may even have to turn out with the Home Guard and be late with his own blue-pencillings. And when all the proofs are at last returned to the printer, our watchful solicitor may decide that one author has shown too great a levity towards a

(Above) *An illustration, 'H.M. Submarines',* *by Eric Ravilious for* Penguin New Writing 22 *(1944).*

distinguished public figure or worthy organ of government; cuts have to be made, but when the printer is hurriedly rung up the Exchange suavely replies: ten hours' delay. Suppose, however, that all is ready to time, the great machines waiting to revolve: the boat with the paper from overseas may have been delayed, and while the machines are idle, the call-up may claim some of the printer's key-workers. Even when the thousands of sheets are safely printed, folded, collated and neatly pressed into their bright new covers, there are plenty of obstacles still lurking: the vans may not get their petrol ration at once, the packers at the warehouse may have decided the week before they would rather fly a Spitfire or man a corvette; and when the parcels have finally been sped from the packing-table to bookshops and bookstalls all over the country, a blitz on the way or sudden war priorities in transport may mean another few days of irritation and disgruntlement to a regular reader. (The Penguin New Writing 8, July 1941)

Yet in spite of these conditions, Penguin achieved a steady flow of fiction and non-fiction titles alongside the ever-increasing new series.

The Penguin Poets series was created in June 1941 with the publication of a selection of works by Tennyson. Poetry had been included under the Pelican imprint from as early as October 1937 with *A Book of English Poetry: Chaucer to Rossetti*, edited by G. B. Harrison, and in the following year two anthologies, *The Centuries' Poetry*, edited by

EDIZIONI DEL PINGUINO

L'ITALIA DI DOMANI

"*L' esempio delle glorie passate, la certezza di non essere soli, il ricordo dei mali patiti per opera del barbaro del nord, la diagnosi della peste fascista che ha infestato e infesta l' Italia, la visione di una società più umana, animeranno a nuovi sacrifici, a nuovi ardimenti, tutti gli italiani che vogliono essere degni del nome che portano.*"

(Above) *The first and only title in the Italian Penguin series,* Edizioni del Pinguino (1942).

Denys Kilham Roberts, were published. These were later removed to the new series as the foundation of a catholic list that steadily developed during the 1950s, 1960s and especially the 1970s, to form the currently available list of well over a hundred titles.

Foreign-language Penguins were launched in 1941 with *Vérités sur la France* by Louis Lévy under the imprint Éditions Pingouin. The six titles were intended for Free French forces and were all on the politics of war, whereas Éditions Penguin, which started in 1944, included titles by Laclos, Diderot, Balzac and Stendhal and were for sale in France until the experiment ended in 1947.

The war undoubtedly affected the emphasis of Penguin's publishing policy. In a letter to a friend in America, Allen Lane described the atmosphere of what was later called the 'phoney war' period, and its influence on his selection of future titles:

There is really an astonishing lack of interest in the whole affair [i.e., the war], and except for the fact that there are more people about in uniform and that there are occasionally slight hitches in getting through supplies, there is very little to denote that there is really a war on. In fact, more and more people are talking of the economic changes which are bound to ensue than they are of the question of winning or being defeated. As far as publishing is concerned, we are switching over very considerably from books on international politics to those discussing the possibility of a new world order when all this mess is over. (Letter from Allen Lane to Mrs Charles Laughton, 1 February 1940)

One striking example of this was Sir Richard Acland's *Unser Kampf*. When published as a Penguin Special in February 1940 it caused such a vocal response amongst readers that Acland was encouraged to form the left-wing Forward March movement, which later merged with J. B. Priestley's 1941 Committee and developed into Common Wealth, an

(Left) *When America joined the war in 1941 and her troops landed in Britain to prepare for the advance on Europe, there was a sudden upsurge of interest in the USA and her people. In response to this, Penguin published a monthly journal,* Transatlantic *(September 1943–June 1946).*

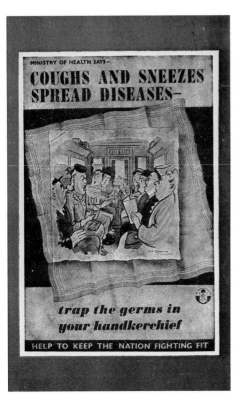

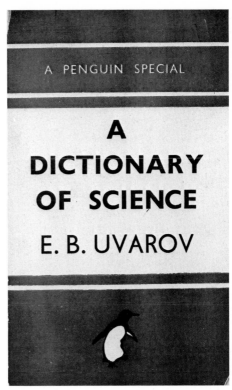

efficient pressure group credited with helping to sweep Labour to victory in the first post-war general election of July 1945.

A less successful example was Professor Lancelot Hogben's *Interglossa*. The author, already well known for his book *Mathematics for the Million* (not published by Penguin), set out to establish a new language based on scientific terms. Penguin's sales leaflet for booksellers declared:

The first printing runs into six figures, and the success or failure of this precedent may well be a guide for future book trade policy. (Penguin Publication List, December 1943)

An indication of its success can be inferred from a remark made by William Emrys Williams at an editorial meeting in December 1946:

Interglossa. *That should be a main exhibit for Penguin's Follies. In a glass case.* (*A Report on Penguin World*, compiled by Mass-Observation (unpublished) 1947)

Perhaps Penguin's ultimate expression of faith in 'a new world order' was the launching

(Above, left) *The back cover of a Penguin Special devoted to the suddenly urgent problem of* Venereal Disease in Britain (1943) *carried the advertisement 'Coughs and sneezes spread diseases'.*

(Above, right) *A Special in 1942,* A Dictionary of Science *led the way for the Reference series, which to date has published over a hundred titles. Five editions and thirty-one reprintings later, this title is still available, not only in English, but in eleven other languages too.*

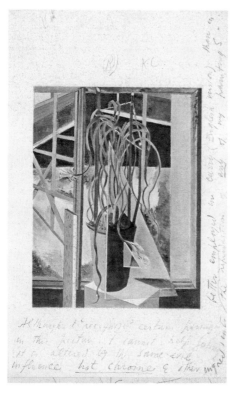

(Above) *Great care was taken to ensure accurate colour reproduction for the Modern Painters. On this proof, the artist, Paul Nash, tried to help the printer by commenting: 'Although I "recognise" certain passages in this picture I cannot help feeling that it is altered by the same evil influence* hot chrome *and other ingredients better employed in curry (English version) than in the reproduction of any of my paintings.'*

EDWARD BAWDEN

The Penguin Modern Painters   Three Shillings and Sixpence

of Penguin Modern Painters just before D-Day 1944. Full-colour and black and white reproductions of paintings and drawings by nineteen leading contemporary artists were published, with helpful introductions, between 1944 and 1959. The Penguin principle of making good contemporary literature readily available as cheaply as possible was being extended to the visual arts:

The Penguin Modern Painters series, edited by Sir Kenneth Clark, was designed to bring the work of painters to the wide public outside the art galleries; the public who have perhaps never ventured within because they doubted their ability to appreciate what they would see.

. . . As the radio has helped the recent remarkable increase in the number of serious concert-goers so the purpose of the Modern Painters series will have been achieved if it disabuses the current idea that modern painting is something unintelligible and that modern Art Galleries are for the few selected initiates. (Penguin's Progress, July 1946)

But possibly Penguin's most significant long-term development occurred in December 1940. Inspired by Soviet Russia's colourfully illustrated books for children, Noel Carrington persuaded Allen Lane to launch Puffin Picture Books, a series of thirty-two-page paperbacks, twice the size of a Penguin at $7 \times 8\frac{3}{4}$ inches (178×222 mm), containing sixteen pages each of four-colour and black and white drawings, selling at sixpence a copy. Noel Carrington said at the time:

I count on the series having a big sale here and a big sale in America. By big I mean millions, or fractions of a million, rather than thousands. I hope Americans will say: 'Well, if the English can produce that in war time for their children and for ours, they are not altogether down and out.' (News Review, 9 January 1941)

Puffin Picture Books were intended to be both entertaining and instructive for children of seven to fourteen. Great care was taken to commission artists and writers who were experts in their subject, such as C. F. Tunni-

(Left) *Between April 1944 and July 1946 over 50,000 copies of the early Modern Painters titles were sold, showing again the public's hunger for culture in a world at war.*

LES MERVEILLES
DU CHARBON

par PEGGY M. HART

COLLECTION DU
VIEUX CHAMOIS

cliffe for *Birds of the Estuary*, Gordon Russell and Jacques Groag for *The Story of Furniture*, and Harold Curwen and J. Brough for *Printing*. S. R. Badmin's *Trees in Britain* inadvertently excelled itself when it became a set text at an agriculture college.

The series was not only an instant success in Britain. Shortly after the war, many titles were translated into other languages, including French, Spanish, Dutch, Hindi, Tamil, Sinhalese and Bahasa Indonesia.

Even when paper rationing was at its height, Puffin Picture Books managed to maintain a publishing programme of ten new books a year, and to start an experimental series of picture books for the very young. Baby Puffin Books cunningly required only half the paper necessary for Picture Books by virtue of reducing by half the size of the book ($4\frac{3}{8} \times 7\frac{1}{8}$ inches). Picture books and fiction for young children, however, were not to become a permanent feature of the Puffin list until Kaye Webb created the astonishingly successful Picture Puffin Books in 1968.

Exactly a year after the start of Puffin Picture Books, in December 1941, Eleanor Graham launched another new children's series called Puffin Story Books. Barbara Euphan Todd's *Worzel Gummidge* led the way, followed during the worst years of the war by such perennials as Eve Garnett's *The Family from One End Street* and Professor J. B. S. Haldane's *My Friend Mr Leakey*. Eleanor Graham recalled twenty-five years later:

. . . that was a difficult time to start anything. The war entailed heavy restrictions on paper and printing; publishers' staffs were depleted, and authors too were scattered on war work. But the

(Above, left) *French Puffin Picture Book,* Les Merveilles du Charbon (The Magic of Coal, *1945*).

(Above) *Illustration from* The Holiday Train Goes to the Moon, *Baby Puffin Books* (*1948*).

(Below) *Scissor-cut illustrations by Lotte Reiniger give great visual impact to Roger Lancelyn Green's popular Puffin Book* King Arthur (*1953*).

The Holiday Train was so surprised at hearing the little man speak that he did not pay any attention to what he said.

first six Puffin Story Books came out that year. They were thin little books, not at all impressive, with red and white covers, and an advertisement for Kiltie Shoes on the back. The printing was good, but the paper was of necessity poor, and it darkened rapidly. ('Twenty-Five Years of Puffins', *The Times Literary Supplement*, 14 April 1966)

During Puffin Story Books' early days, the editor had great difficulty in persuading

(Above) *Originally published as a Penguin Special in December 1942, this title was quickly transferred to start yet another new series, Penguin Handbooks.*

hardback publishers to release the rights to many of the important works she wanted to see in paperback at a price children could afford from their pocket money. Resisting the temptation to publish the lesser works offered, Eleanor Graham kept the list small – never exceeding more than a dozen titles a year between 1941 and 1961 – thereby giving Puffin Story Books the reputation for publishing the best books available: *The Incredible Adventures of Professor Branestawm* (1947) by Norman Hunter, *Redcap Runs Away* (1957) by Rhoda Power, *The Borrowers* (1958) by Mary Norton, and *Tomorrow is a New Day* (1949), Jennie Lee's autobiography about her climb out of poverty in a mining village to her gaining a seat in Parliament, and so on. These were complemented by specially commissioned titles such as Kitty Barne's biography *Elizabeth Fry* (1950), Eve Garnett's illustrated edition of Robert Louis Stevenson's *A Child's Garden of Verses* (1948), and Roger Lancelyn Green's *King Arthur* (1953).

By the end of the war, Penguin's volume output was less than half the amount it had been prior to paper rationing, but its policy of diversity had succeeded in establishing it in the minds of the general public and the book trade as a publisher of good books for all tastes and all ages, from popular novels and short stories to the latest scientific theories, from poetry and plays to practical guides on rearing rabbits and cultivating fruit trees, from comparative religion to tales for children, from detective fiction to art criticism, from political theories to philosophical treatises. The nervous tension and continuous flow of adrenalin that pulled the nation through the war was reflected in the energy with which Allen Lane and his few remaining staff achieved the production of hundreds of titles on every conceivable subject.

1946–59

'All the survivors of the war had reached their homes by now and so put the perils of battle and the sea behind them.'*

The wave of euphoria that swept over the country when war ended was shortlived. The nation was exhausted; strict rationing remained in force; skilled labour was in short supply; and the worst weather for a hundred years created a food and fuel crisis throughout Europe during the winter of 1946/7.

Although the demand for books fell sharply to near pre-war levels, Penguin was still unable to fulfil all orders. Exports suffered as the home market's quota system received priority, and orders from abroad were dealt with on a rota basis, with one country receiving its supplies one month, another country the next month:

> We've got a consignment of books stuck in the River Magdalena. The only way to reach Bogota is up the river, it is inaccessible by land. And halfway up the river dried up and the steamer is stuck in the mud. So we've no books and no money. (A Report on Penguin World, compiled by Mass-Observation (unpublished), 1947)

Exports to America dwindled to a trickle during the war, but the name of Penguin was kept alive there by Penguin Books Inc., which was formed in July 1939. Ian Ballantine and his wife Betty constituted the firm's vice president, secretary and treasurer. Between them, they established Penguin in New York, distributed what books they could obtain from Britain, and began publishing American Penguins. Ballantine came to an arrangement with the *Infantry Journal* whereby they would provide Penguin with sufficient paper (rationed when America entered the war in

(Above) Penguin's Progress, *a free booklet announcing forthcoming titles, soon picked up the firm's wide pre-war distribution. But post-war shortages still severely disrupted publishing schedules. Bob Hill, head of Cash Sales, had to deal with disappointed and irate customers, and at the end of 1946 was overheard to declare despairingly, 'Penguin's Progress is like a work of fiction.'*

*Homer, *The Odyssey*, translated by E. V. Rieu, Penguin Books, 1946.

43

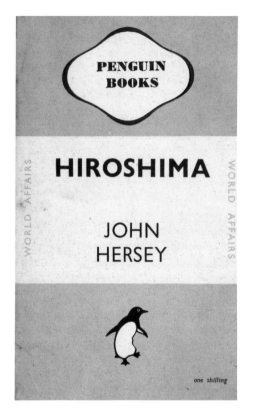

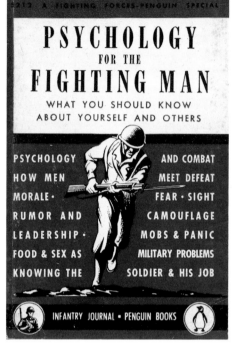

(Above) *John Hersey's 30,000-word essay on the tragic effects of the atomic bomb dropped on Hiroshima on Monday, 6 August 1945, was published in the* New Yorker *magazine just twelve months later. Penguin immediately bought the rights, and published 250,000 copies in Britain on Armistice Day 1946. One West End bookshop reported it to be selling at a rate of a hundred copies an hour.*

(Above, right) *By the end of the war, Penguin Books Inc. was said to be distributing up to one million books a month, a phenomenal output for a new company operating under difficult conditions.*

December 1941) if Penguin would publish titles the editor of the *Journal* deemed useful to the war effort. Both contemporary novels and such titles as *How the Jap Army Fights* by Four US Army Officers, *Guerrilla Warfare* by 'Yank' Levy, and *G.I. Sketch Book* edited by Aimée Crane were purchased in large quantities by the US Army and the general public.

There was as much prejudice in America against paperbacks in 1939 as there had been in Britain when Penguin started in 1935:

When Betty and I began we were told that paperbound books must fail because reading paperbound books was something that Europeans do but that Americans would never do! (Letter from Ian Ballantine to Linda Lloyd Jones, 28 September 1984)

Ballantine believes that it was the regular supply of Armed Services editions – the very first of which was a Penguin *Infantry Journal* reprint of John Steinbeck's *The Moon is Down* – to the fighting forces that totally changed American attitudes towards paperbacks.

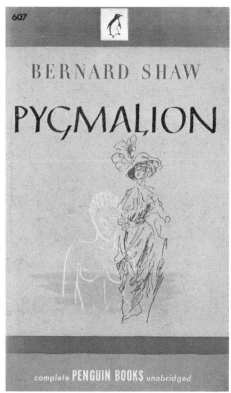

Kurt Enoch, co-founder in 1931 of Germany's English-language Albatross Modern Continental Library (the design of which inspired the format Penguin adopted in 1935), joined Ballantine and his team of two salesmen and a part-time accountant at the end of 1941. Enoch's experience with the European paperback series gave Penguin Books Inc. in America the additional expertise necessary to operate independently of Penguin at Harmondsworth, ensuring its survival while communications between the two countries were so difficult. At the end of the war, however, Allen Lane wanted Penguin Books Inc. to revert to a selective publishing policy and not enter the field of 'popular' publishing which American companies like Pocket Books (also founded in 1939), Avon, Dell and Popular Library had all successfully pursued during the war. Ian Ballantine left to set up Bantam Books, and Allen Lane's senior editor, Eunice Frost, temporarily joined Kurt Enoch to re-establish Penguin Inc.'s identity as a

(Above, left) *Victor Weybright alleged that on Penguin Inc.'s publication of Erskine Caldwell's novel* God's Little Acre *Allen Lane remarked that the company should not be called Penguin Books, but Porno Books. Caldwell's book sold over a million copies in six months.*

To celebrate Bernard Shaw's ninetieth birthday in July 1946, Penguin simultaneously published in Britain 100,000 copies each of ten of his works, using the standard tripartite cover design. On publication day queues were reported outside bookshops. The entire million copies were sold within six weeks.

Three of the ten Shaw titles, bearing pictorial covers, including Pygmalion (above), *were published in America by Penguin Inc. Weybright suggested to Shaw's American hardback publishers, Dodd, Mead, that Penguin should therefore be invited to their celebratory dinner at the Waldorf Astoria. They replied, 'Penguin should have their own celebrations – at the Automat.'*

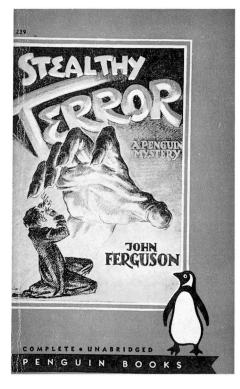

(Above) *One of the first American Penguin
Specials,* What's That Plane, *was written by
Walter Pitkin, Penguin Inc.'s first editor; his
wife Suzanne traced the silhouettes from
drawings provided by the British Information
Service; Ian Ballantine designed the cover; and
his wife, Betty, did the layouts. Large numbers
of the book were purchased by the US Army.*

(Above, right) *Busoni created a suitably
terrifying image for this American Penguin
Mystery title. Such a Penguin cover would have
been unthinkable in Britain in 1940.*

publisher of quality fiction and to launch an
American Pelican imprint.

Convinced that Penguin's more specialized
titles would sell in mass-market outlets such as
drugstores and news-stands, as long as they
were not swamped by the more 'popular'
paperbacks, Enoch assiduously travelled the
country persuading wholesalers to give Penguin special displays in educational, cultural
and 'heavy traffic' outlets, as well as calling on
bookshops in an attempt to reconcile them to
paperbacks. As Penguin Inc.'s revenue came
mainly from 'non-bookshops' where titles are
bought on impulse from a display, Enoch was
acutely aware of the importance of an eye-
catching cover. He was equally aware that
they could be 'in bad taste, corny or worse . . .'
(*Memoirs of Kurt Enoch*, New York, 1984). His
solution was to commission the best commercial artists to present the books' contents
in an interesting and attractive way.

In December 1945, Victor Weybright joined
Penguin Inc. and fearlessly extended the
fiction list to include William Faulkner, Erskine
Caldwell, James T. Farrell and James M. Cain.
For Allen Lane, the combination of authors he
then regarded as risqué, illustrated covers
which had always been anathema to him, and
the American practice of sending out books
on 'sale or return' was beyond endurance for
a company bearing the name of Penguin.
Lawyers were summoned, and at the end of
January 1948 the link between the United

Kingdom and the United States was severed. Enoch and Weybright went on to form the successful New American Library of World Literature, and Penguin Inc. was reconstituted in January 1950 under Harry Paroissien, an Englishman with many years' experience in the British book trade.

Initially, the new Penguin Books Inc. distributed only British Penguin titles. The American book trade at this time considered Allen Lane's publishing philosophy as conservative, and had even described Penguin's cover designs as 'puritanical'. But the renewed attempt to enter the American market did receive from some quarters the kind of welcome Allen Lane wanted:

The cheap reprints most widely available at present are 95 per cent sheer trash. We've had enough of fancy jackets and profane displays. These Penguins won't undermine the American publisher. They are a fine contribution to the book world. They'll whet the literary appetite of the man who has left school. They'll improve the public taste. And they'll give the serious publishers an

economic jolt which should hasten the return of book prices to a dollar's worth for a dollar – a state of affairs which would benefit us all. (Interview with Siegfried Weisberger, a Charles Street bookseller, *Baltimore Sun*, 17 January 1950)

The New York based *Publishers Weekly* joined in the debate:

The covers on many of the 25 cent fiction currently issued, from the point of view of taste, seem to get worse . . . The pocket series have opened

(Below, left) *Published in Britain in June 1949,* Popular Art in the United States *was amongst the first books promoted by the reconstituted Penguin Books Inc.*

(Below) *A comment by Gilbert Highet on Penguin was taken up as a promotional slogan in the United States: 'Not one of the Penguin books has a cover which emphasizes the fact that human beings are mammals. On the contrary, they treat us as intellectuals.'*

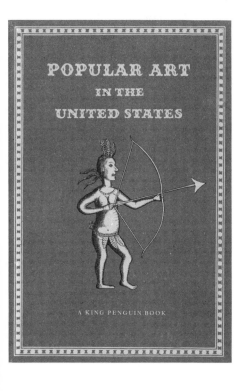

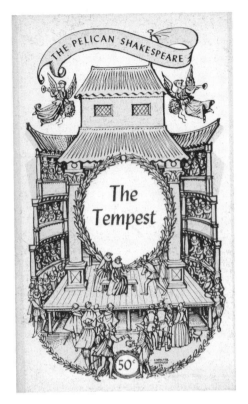

(Above) *By the mid-1950s more than half Penguin's annual sales of ten million books were exported. Khrushchev's Russia was a Penguin bestseller in America in 1959.*

(Above) *The Pelican Shakespeare series, launched in 1956, was the first independent publishing venture of the re-formed American company. 'Some of the texts are perhaps the best available at any price . . . Its text and its apparatus (and its handsome format) combine to put it ahead of all the rest' (College English, USA, March 1961).*

(Left) *Harry F. Paroissien and a staff of four re-formed Penguin Books Inc. at Clipper Mill Road, Woodbury, Maryland, in a building once used by the sailmakers of the famous Baltimore clippers.*

a great supplemental market for books. The way to this market was first pointed out in Europe with the Albatross and the Penguin series, and the Penguins have been able to keep up a quantity production without resorting to suggestive covers for fiction . . . There is a profitable market on our newsstands without a specious sex appeal featured on the cover and a subtitle which often has little relation to the text . . . Guns can blaze on westerns, but in such fiction not every woman needs to be pictured with torn clothes . . . Their publishers will be lucky if the current displays are not pointed at – rightly or wrongly – as partly responsible for sex crimes and juvenile delinquency . . . The popular price market is an important one and has a diversified public. Reading matter of permanent value, for recreation, and to give practical information is being made available for all. It is a market that should not be fouled up by directing a mass appeal to its least stable elements.
(Publishers Weekly, 29 April 1950)

But Penguin's selective publishing and sober cover designs did not compete successfully with the other American mass-market paperbacks. Instead, Paroissien decided to develop a specialized market for Penguin Classics. Orders from schools and colleges made Homer's *The Odyssey* Penguin Inc.'s bestseller for 1952, along with *The Canterbury Tales* and Dorothy L. Sayers's translation of Dante's *Hell*. By 1960 nearly 2 million Penguin books were being sold annually in America, half of them for educational use.

'NO CARS, NO HOUSES, NO BEER, NO CIGARETTES, NO PETROL, NO WAREHOUSE SPACE'
(Bob Maynard: *Memoirs* (unpublished), 1984)

Australia, unlike America, was materially affected by the war. 'No Cars, No Houses, No Beer, No Cigarettes, No Petrol, No Warehouse Space,' recalls Bob Maynard, who was personally responsible for setting up Penguin Books Australia in August 1946.

Penguins had been on sale in Australia right from the start, as they had been in many other countries, thanks to contacts made by John, Allen Lane's youngest brother, on his tour of the world in 1934 as The Bodley Head's export manager. The three brothers had that year divided up the job of persuading booksellers to try out their new type of book:

(Above) *John Lane calculated in 1938 that Penguin's best export markets were India, Holland, New Zealand, Australia and South Africa – with Japan following close behind.* (BBC Hulton Picture Library.)

(Below) *With the prospect of the first African colony, Ghana, gaining independence in 1957, the West African series was initiated in 1953.*

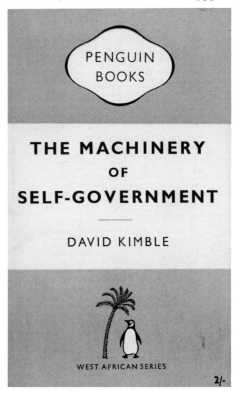

John looked after the export sales as he knew hundreds of booksellers throughout the world and had visited their shops. Instead of sending them a specimen copy and asking them to send him an order, he wrote and told them he was forwarding a certain number of Penguins as he knew they could sell them. This method of selling proved to be 100 per cent successful. (Richard Lane: *Memoirs* (unpublished), 1971)

Indeed, John Lane's overseas contacts accounted for as much as 10 per cent of Penguin's initial orders in 1935. Two years later almost one third of the ten million books sold had gone abroad.

Bob Maynard rejoined Penguin at Harmondsworth when the war came to an end. To his delight, he was immediately despatched by Allen Lane to 'survey the scene "down under"'.

He arrived in Australia in May 1946 to find the country 'short of everything except food and goodwill'.

The bank manager found me a beer ration and a cigarette ration. The solicitor found half a tin shed in Normanby Road, South Melbourne. I could not afford to travel the country to show the flag, but the press did a good job on my behalf, all of which led to the bank being convinced that a loan was in order. (Bob Maynard: Memoirs (unpublished), 1984)

Penguins started to arrive from Harmondsworth towards the end of 1946. Maynard could not afford to pay staff to distribute the books, but with the help of his wife working on

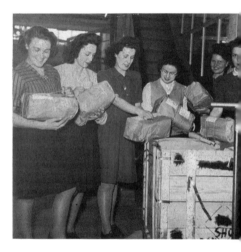

(Above, right) *Penguin Australia's first office/warehouse in Melbourne, 1946.*

(Centre, right) *Rationing in Britain continued long after the war, and in 1948 Australian booksellers donated profits from the sale of John Hersey's harrowing book,* Hiroshima, *to the Hiroshima Food for Britain Fund. Penguin staff at Harmondsworth received a share.*

(Below, right) *Penguin Australia rapidly outgrew its tin shed in Melbourne, and in 1953 work began on a new office and warehouse at Mitcham. The sign announcing building work caused some confusion amongst local animal lovers.*

A SANCTUARY FOR PENGUINS AND PELICANS
IS BEING ERECTED ON THIS SITE
BY JOHN HOLLAND & CO PTY LTD.
ENGINEERS & MASTER BUILDERS
28 HAUGHTON Rd.   OAKLEIGH

(Above) *Australia's Patrick White won the 1959 W. H. Smith Literary Award for* Voss.

(Above) *This book, published in 1970, is in Penguin Australia's bestseller list, beside George Orwell's 1984.*

the packing bench, he managed to sell over four hundred thousand Penguins, Pelicans and Puffins in the first year. In July 1948, *Penguin's Progress*, the firm's free publication announcing new titles, informed readers:

There is a two-way purpose involved in setting up the Australian Penguin company. Its immediate business is to secure an increasing flow of books into the Dominion and to ensure that the remoter inhabitants, no less than the citizens of the big towns, get their portion of good reading. But it is hoped that Australia will yield books as well as absorb them. As a young country with a great future Australia wants the world to know more about its achievements and potentialities. In science, art and literature it has many notable figures – such as Dobell and Drysdale, who will appear in Modern Painters before long. (Penguin's Progress, July 1948)

Neither Dobell nor Drysdale was destined to

appear in the Modern Painters series before it ceased publication in 1950. Indeed Penguin's good intentions towards Australian authors were not to come to fruition until March 1963, when Penguin Australia published just three titles, *To the Islands* by Randolph Stow, *Kangaroo Tales* edited by Rosemary Wighton, and *Three Australian Plays*. The list has grown steadily in recent years, however, under Trevor Glover and Brian Johns. By 1983 Puffin Books accounted for 49 per cent of all children's books sold in Australia. In 1985, Australian authors have over 500 Penguin titles available in the southern hemisphere, including literary figures such as Patrick White, Thomas Keneally, Elizabeth Jolley, Albert Facey, David Malouf, David Ireland and Henry Handel Richardson, combining to generate nearly 25 per cent of Penguin Australia's annual turnover.

'As a publisher he has proved himself to be a genius . . . as a financier Mr Lane has also proved himself to be a very astute man of business because somehow or other he has persuaded Martins Bank to finance him in a manner which normally no joint stock bank would dream of doing.' (Financial report on Penguin by the company's accountants, Messrs James E. Ward and Sons, 31 January 1949)

Not until the end of 1960 did Penguin's annual sales pick up to the level achieved in 1941. The company's rapid growth before the war, combined with wartime paper rationing, labour shortages and an Excess Profits Tax, as well as post-war inflation, meant that, although remaining profitable, Penguin relied heavily upon the goodwill of its bankers to maintain that essential business ingredient – cash flow. But Allen Lane succeeded in juggling his desire for expansion abroad with his lack of capital for investment by employing staff prepared to take on a challenge.

Harry Paroissien had £3,000 with which to set up in America in 1950, and Bob Maynard

(Below) *A. S. B. Glover was the firm's senior editor responsible for Pelicans and Penguin Classics from 1944 to 1960. He is reputed to have written so often to Penguin, pointing out textual or printing errors, that Allen Lane offered him the job.*

(Above) *Alan Ross's invention of the classifications 'U' and 'Non-U' first appeared in* Encounter *magazine in 1956. They eventually entered popular English vocabulary after the much wider distribution provided by Penguin's* Noblesse Oblige, *edited by Nancy Mitford (1959).*

had just £100 in travellers cheques when he arrived in Australia in 1946.

Such financial precariousness did not, however, prevent Allen Lane from taking calculated risks. The Classics had been launched in 1946 with E. V. Rieu's translation of Homer's *The Odyssey*. Dr Rieu had developed the evening pastime of translating aloud to his wife so that she too could enjoy the books that so absorbed him. At her suggestion he wrote down his version of *The Odyssey*, and when the war ended, he presented the manuscript to Penguin. There was a heated debate amongst editorial board members about the desirability of yet another translation: there were already several other editions available in English, and

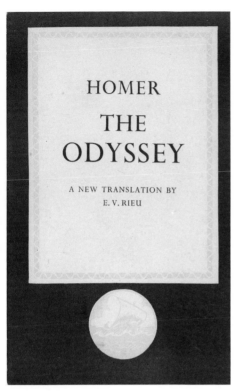

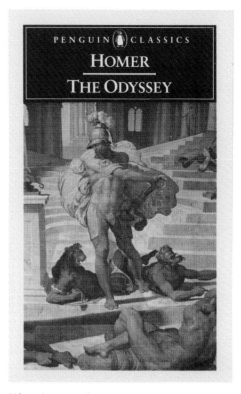

(Above) *Penguin's first edition of Homer's* Odyssey *(1946). 'Reading neither Greek nor Latin, I was stunned by what is to me a new way of experiencing* The Odyssey' *(extract from a letter to Dr Rieu from a Penguin reader, S. Glowacki, New Haven, Connecticut, 5 April 1950).*

(Above) *Penguin's 1985 edition of* The Odyssey. *Nearly three million copies have been sold since the first Penguin edition thirty-nine years ago – probably more than the sum total of every volume of* The Odyssey *produced since Homer wrote it in the eighth century* BC.

none was reputed to have sold more than 3,000 copies. Allen Lane ignored the advice and insisted that *The Odyssey* should not only be accepted but that Rieu be appointed to commission translations of other classics to form a new series. *The Odyssey*'s spectacular success surpassed even Allen Lane's expectations. Reviewers and readers alike praised the book:

In the world of books something important has happened – more interesting than the publication of a shelf full of bestsellers. There is a new translation of The Odyssey, *a very contemporary translation, and it costs only one shilling. This is revolutionary . . . It is* The Odyssey *very much as a novel, still with all the oceanic surge but without*

some of the thunder. Almost colloquial but sinewy and of our own experience. (Reynolds' News, January 1946)

Never before in my life, dogged by unhappy bouts with Latin, did I suspect that anything 'classical' could give me real pleasure . . . Thank you for opening my eyes to what must have been the essential quality of the minds of those ancient people. (Letter to Dr Rieu from H. D. Adams, Director, Junior Art Gallery Inc., Louisville Kentucky Free Public Library, 8 April 1950)

The Odyssey rapidly became Penguin's bestselling book; it was only eclipsed in 1961 by *Lady Chatterley's Lover.*

Rieu went on to translate Virgil's *Pastoral Poems*, Homer's *The Iliad*, *The Four Gospels* and

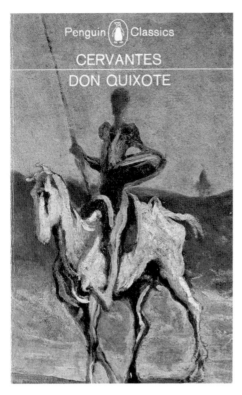

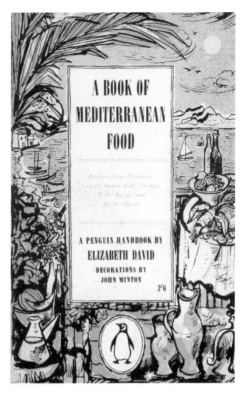

(Above) *From 1950 to 1964 J. M. Cohen
supervised the modern-language Penguin Classics
and translated some of them himself, including*
Don Quixote *(1950), shown here in the 1978
edition.*

(Above) *Elizabeth David's* Book of
Mediterranean Food *(1955) was written while
food rationing still made some ingredients a
luxury and others a dream of future prosperity.*

Apollonius of Rhodes's *The Voyage of Argo*.
When he retired as series editor in 1964 there
were over 130 Penguin Classics titles selling
nearly a million copies a year.

In Britain throughout the 1950s, Specials
on politics and social issues remained dormant, perhaps because the population was
preoccupied with reconstructing the country
and re-creating a home life. The Handbooks
series, on domestic subjects from *Beekeeping*
and *The Flower Garden* to *The Penguin Knitting
Book* and *The Art of Marriage*, proliferated
within a series begun during the war to aid the
'Dig for Victory' campaign.

As well as successfully encouraging self-
sufficiency at home, Penguin made a sterling
effort to interest readers in good design and art.
In the years up to and following the Festival of
Britain (1951), expert opinions and advice

were offered by Hugh Casson in *Homes by the
Million*, Bertil Hultén in *Building Modern
Sweden*, Ruhemann and Kemp in *The Artist at
Work*, John Walker in *Paintings from America*,
Gordon Russell in *Furniture* and Bernard
Hollowood in *Pottery and Glass*.

Under the general heading of 'Planning,
Design and Art', The Things We See series
endeavoured to:
*encourage us to look at objects of everyday life with
fresh and critical eyes . . . To achieve this in the
furnishing and equipment of our homes, we must
buy with discrimination and so prove to the
designers, who set the machines to work, that we
are no longer bound by habit or indifference to
accept whatever is offered.* (Publicity blurb for
The Things We See series, December 1947)

Despite official backing from the Council of
Industrial Design and support from William

(Above) *Emett's* The Festival Railway, *a Puffin Cut-Out Book, was specially published in 1951 to coincide with the Festival of Britain exhibition, at which he had constructed a life-size track, train and carriages. There were ten Puffin Cut-Out Books in the series, including* The High Toby *by J. B. Priestley.*

(Above and below) *Conceived in 1945, Penguin Prints were dogged by shortages of materials and skilled technicians. Picasso's* Le Chardonneret *advertised the launch of Penguin Prints, and in December 1948 John Piper's* View of Windsor Castle *was one of the first four published. Selling at six shillings each (including two shillings Purchase Tax) they were remarkable value for full colour reproductions of famous artists' works. Eleven prints appeared between 1948 and 1952.*

(Below) *The desire for Britain to reconstruct a new and better environment was reflected in the planning, design and art books that appeared in the early post-war years.*

Emrys Williams, a founder member of the Arts Council of Great Britain, the British public remained unmoved by arguments for aesthetic awareness, and all publishing within the planning, design and art series, including Penguin Modern Painters and Penguin Prints, largely ceased in the early 1950s. None the less, William Emrys Williams described the Festival of Britain as 'the renaissance of the arts' (*Penguin's Progress 14*, 1951), and he must have considered Penguin's publishing as a major contribution to this rebirth. In retrospect, perhaps the most significant was the publication of the first volumes in The Buildings of England series. The German *émigré* art historian, Nikolaus Pevsner, persuaded Allen Lane that a county-by-county series of architectural guidebooks of a high academic standard at a low cost was sorely needed. With the help of two part-time assistants and a secretary, Professor Pevsner undertook to research and write the forty-six-volume series during his university vacations. Penguin lent him a 1933 Wolseley Hornet (along with a permit for thirty gallons of rationed petrol) for the first county tour in 1947. Mrs Pevsner acted as chauffeur, helping her husband keep to the rigorous schedule of rising at 6 am to visit buildings by day and writing up the first draft of the guide late into each night. The forty-sixth and final volume was published in 1974, twenty-three years after the first. Pevsner wrote thirty-two of them – a remarkable feat of stamina and determination. Over the twenty-three years, however, the costs of research and production rose dramatically while sales remained relatively static. As the aim of the series was to make architectural guides available at prices most people could afford, Penguin was forced to seek financial help towards the research. The Leverhulme Trust, Arthur Guinness and Son, ABC Television and the GLC have all made generous donations towards The Buildings of England, thereby ensuring completion and the continued revision of a series which has become accepted as the standard work on Britain's architectural heritage: 'Mentioned in Pevsner' is now almost a required reference for planners and architectural historians.

Pevsner's other major contribution to the Penguin backlist was as editor of The Pelican History of Art. When the first four volumes

(Above) *Nikolaus Pevsner with his monumental series, The Buildings of England.*

appeared in 1953 – *Painting in Britain: 1530–1790* by Ellis Waterhouse, *The Art and Architecture of India: Hindu, Buddhist, Jain* by Benjamin Rowland, *Architecture in Britain: 1530–1830* by John Summerson and *Art and Architecture in France: 1500–1700* by Anthony Blunt – Penguin announced that forty-eight volumes would appear within twelve years, each to be written by:

a European or American scholar recognized as an outstanding specialist in his subject. A revealing aside on the quality of the contributors was made by The Times Literary Supplement *in its special issue of August 1952, devoted to the general theme of 'Fresh Minds at Work', when it commented on the dearth of recent contributions to art in the following terms: 'The comparative paucity of important publications can be explained by the obvious fact that the processes of scholarship are long, but there is another reason, The Pelican History of Art is monopolizing many of our leading authorities.'* (Penguin publicity leaflet 'Announcing The Pelican History of Art', 15 May 1953)

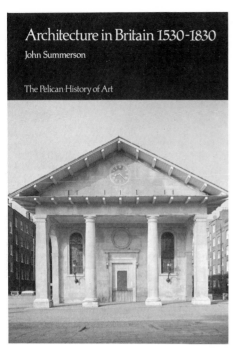

Architecture in Britain 1530-1830
John Summerson

The Pelican History of Art

(Above) *John Summerson has revised his book six times since 1953 to ensure that the most recent research is made available. The 1983 paperback edition is shown here. By 1985 forty-four Pelican History of Art volumes had been published. Another sixteen are planned.*

The 'processes of scholarship' have indeed proved to be long: the series has taken not twelve but thirty years to reach forty-four of the predicted forty-eight volumes. At least one author died before delivering his manuscript; another laboured for seventeen years to complete his work; and a third delivered his manuscript so long before his co-author that he was compelled to revise the work in typescript to accommodate new research before it ever saw the light of day.

At the opposite end of the spectrum from those weighty works of reference were the periodicals on film, music, biology, science and Russian affairs that Penguin experimented with in the late 1940s and throughout the 1950s. Many magazines went to the wall during the war and new ones were banned from starting up while paper rationing lasted. In the guise of books, *Film Review* (1946–9),

Music Magazine (1947–9), *New Biology* (1945–60), *Russian Review* (1945–8), and *Science News* (1946–60) were published with varying degrees of success. The most popular periodicals were *New Biology* and *Science News*, which were

started with the avowed intention of keeping the intelligent layman abreast of what is going on in research laboratories. (Penguin's Progress, October 1946)

Penguin enjoyed unchallenged supremacy in the field of paperbacks throughout the 1950s. There had been attempts to cash in on the cheap reprint market by many firms including Hutchinsons, Collins, Cherry Tree Books and even a consortium of publishers forming Guild Books, prior to and during the war, but Penguin held itself above the rest as a publisher of reliable, authoritative books which,

if the vicar called, you wouldn't hide under the cushion, but you'd even put them on the table in order to let people see what kind of person you

(Below) *The periodical* Russian Review *was intended to familiarize Britons with their new allies.*

RUSSIAN REVIEW

ONE SHILLING

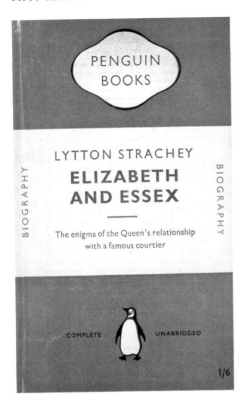

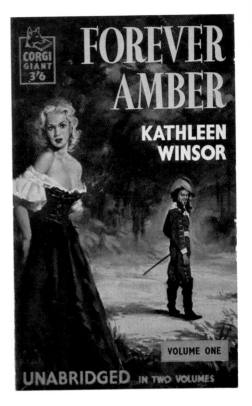

(Above) *First published in Penguin in 1948 under the 'group agreement', Lytton Strachey's psychological melodrama,* Elizabeth and Essex, *remains in the Penguin backlist.*

(Above, right) *Corgi's* Forever Amber *(1957). 'More than fifty million British paper-backed books are being sold every year from 44,000 display points in Great Britain and throughout the Commonwealth' (Printing News, 27 December 1956).*

(Opposite page, top left) *Pan's* The Colditz Story, *1954. By 1958 at least 3,000 titles were being issued a year in paperback by over twenty-five publishers.*

were. (Allen Lane in a BBC interview, 'Frankly Speaking', 1 February 1961)

Such a clear identity increased reader and author loyalty to the extent that the name 'Penguin' became synonymous with the term 'paperback'.

Serious competition began to affect Penguin's sales only when, in June 1947, Alan Bott started up Pan Books with financial backing from the hardback publishers Collins, Macmillan, Heinemann and Hodder and Stoughton. Allen Lane quickly responded in the autumn of 1947 by announcing a 'group agreement' with Chatto and Windus, Faber and Faber, Hamish Hamilton, Heinemann and Michael Joseph, five leading publishers who undertook to offer Penguin first refusal on all their leading authors' works. This arrangement immensely strengthened Penguin's literary list, starting in July 1948 with Lytton Strachey's *Eminent Victorians*, Aldous Huxley's *Antic Hay*, Somerset Maugham's *Cakes and Ale* and J. B. Priestley's *Angel Pavement*.

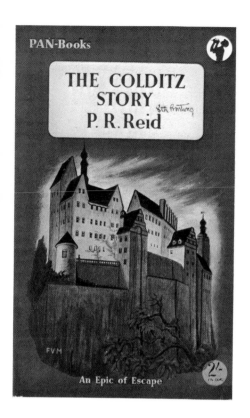

(Above) *In March 1950 a hundred thousand copies each of ten titles by D. H. Lawrence were published simultaneously, making another Penguin Million.*

But in spite of Penguin's broad and innovative publishing, the majority of books sold, as in previous and future decades, were fiction titles from authors as diverse as Graham Greene and Monica Dickens, F. Scott Fitzgerald and Georgette Heyer, Arnold Bennett and Angela Thirkell. The 1950s, however, were dominated by readers' insatiable appetite for the famous green and white jacketed crime books. Detective fiction by such writers as Margery Allingham, Carter Dickson, Georges Simenon, John Dickson Carr, Erle Stanley Gardner, Agatha Christie, Rex Stout, Ngaio Marsh, Ellery Queen, Michael Innes and others accounted for an astonishing 25 per cent of all fiction published by Penguin between 1950 and 1960, and by 1961 represented 33 per cent of all Penguin fiction in print. These masters of mystery not only kept their fans guessing 'who dunnit' but enabled Penguin to survive the difficult transition period from post-war austerity to the affluence of the 1960s.

(Below) *Advertisements for the famous green and white crime series (December 1946 and March 1949).*

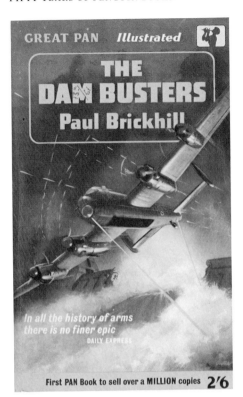

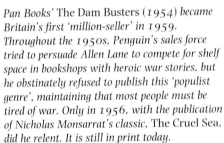

Pan Books' The Dam Busters *(1954) became Britain's first 'million-seller' in 1959. Throughout the 1950s, Penguin's sales force tried to persuade Allen Lane to compete for shelf space in bookshops with heroic war stories, but he obstinately refused to publish this 'populist genre', maintaining that most people must be tired of war. Only in 1956, with the publication of Nicholas Monsarrat's classic,* The Cruel Sea, *did he relent. It is still in print today.*

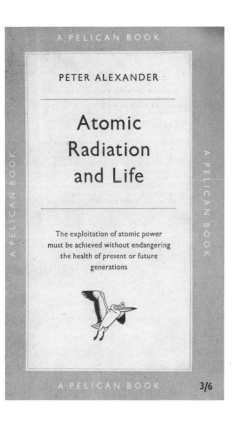

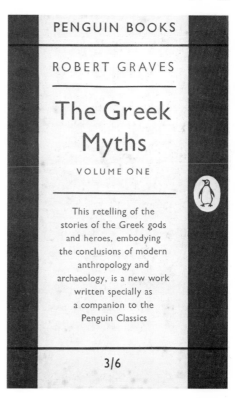

By 1956, more than half of Penguin's titles published each year were, then as now, originals and not reprints – the staple diet of other emerging paperback houses. William Emrys Williams stated in The Penguin Story (1956), perhaps a little imperiously, 'the freelance phase of Penguins is over; the adventurous sallies have given way to the solid responsibility of building up a comprehensive Popular Educator.'

(Above) *Perhaps the single most telling example
of the strength of Penguin's backlist are the
works of George Orwell, all in print for many
years.
When BBC Television transmitted the film
of Orwell's 1984 one weekend in December
1954, Penguin was amazed by the public
response. There were 18,000 copies of the book
in the warehouse on the Monday morning. By
Wednesday it was 'out of stock'.*

(Above, right) Gigi, *first in Penguin in 1958,
was given a new cover bearing a photograph from
the film. Twenty-six thousand copies of the
'tie-in' cover edition were sold during the first
month of the film's release in Britain in 1959.
Film and TV tie-ins had come to stay.*

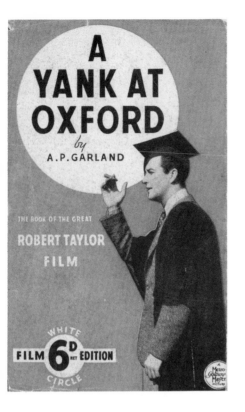

(Above, left) A Yank at Oxford, *published in
1938 by Collins under the White Circle imprint,
must be one of the earliest 'film tie-ins'. Until the
1960s, film companies paid the publisher for
using a film-still on the book cover. Today,
publishers vie with one another to buy the tie-in
rights from the film-makers.*

(Above) *Following the nation's addiction to the
science fiction series* The Quatermass
Experiment *on B B C Television, Penguin
published Nigel Kneale's script in 1959, making
'the book of the film'.*

(Above) *'Many concert-goers and wireless listeners find that their satisfaction is increased by following the score as they attend to the performance, and these will welcome the news that we are beginning to publish a series of*

Penguin Pocket Scores at the price of half-a-crown each' (Penguin's Progress 8, Spring 1949). *Thirty scores, measuring $5\frac{1}{8} \times 7\frac{3}{4}$ inches (127×197 mm), were published between June 1949 and April 1956.*

PENGUIN BOOKS

ERIC LINKLATER
Private Angelo

'The drollest medley of muddle and misadventure in Southern Europe'
Sunday Times

COMPLETE **2/6** UNABRIDGED

(Left) *Print-runs of 40,000 to 50,000 copies per title were necessary to keep unit costs down to Allen Lane's desired price. As the number of books published grew year by year, so did the amount of capital tied up in slow-selling stock. Finally it became urgent to produce small quantities and reprint more often. Keeping metal type standing ready for reprints was costly, so in conjunction with McCorquodale, the London printers, Penguin made printing history in December 1957 by becoming the first publisher in England to produce a book entirely without metal type. Eric Linklater's* Private Angelo *was composed on Intertype Fotosetter, the rubber plates being easily stored, ready at any time for reprinting. (The paperback edition was published in March 1958.)*

1960–69

'Let's be frank about it; most of our people
have never had it so good.
Go around the country, go to the industrial towns,
go to the farms and you will see
a state of prosperity such as we have never had
in my lifetime –
nor indeed ever in the history of this country.'*

The furore surrounding the trial of *Lady Chatterley's Lover* catapulted Penguin into the decade that fostered 'the permissive society'. D. H. Lawrence's novel was acquitted of the charge that it would 'tend to deprave and corrupt' in the first case to be heard under the newly passed Obscene Publications Act (1959). The press had a field-day. Counsel for the Prosecution maintained that the book:

sets on a pedestal promiscuous intercourse, commends sensuality almost as a virtue, and encourages and even advocates coarseness and vulgarity of thought and language.

He went on, perhaps fatally for his case:

Would you approve of your young sons and daughters – because girls can read as well as boys – reading this book? Is it a book you would have lying around in your own house? Is it a book you would even wish your wife or your servants to read?

The week-long trial was fully reported by 'the top people's paper' and the popular press alike. The tabloids indulged in cartoons and expurgated extracts while *The Times* leader writer warned:

A decent reticence has been the practice in all classes of society and much will be lost by the destruction of it.

(Above) *The nation was agog to discover what the Crown felt was unsuitable for its eyes. Massive pre-trial publicity ensured a packed public gallery at the famous Number One Court, the Old Bailey (Guardian Journal, 28 October 1960).*

Penguin sold two million copies of *Lady Chatterley's Lover* in the six weeks up to Christmas 1960, and a further one million three hundred thousand copies during 1961. If ever proof were needed that publicity makes a million-seller, the trial of *Lady Chatterley* provided it.

Sir Allen Lane's sense of personal triumph at winning the case may, after forty years in publishing, have given him the signal to relinquish the day-to-day responsibilities of

*Harold Macmillan, Prime Minister, speaking at Bedford, 20 July 1957.

(Below) *Front page of the* Daily Sketch, *3 November 1960.*

(Above) *In a review of the decade, Malcolm Muggeridge reported: 'An abortive Summit Conference with full supporting cast is soon forgotten; police court proceedings about a book –* Lady Chatterley's Lover – *which at the time caused more hilarity than serious consideration, affect our way of life more than ever* Magna Carta *did'* (Observer Magazine, *December 1969).*

(Left) *'Lady Chatterley's Lover? Listen, mate, if that's the book that's so pure and decent it's even fit for schoolgirls to read then we don't stock it'* (Sprod in Punch, *9 November 1960).*

(Right) *'I've been feeling terribly sub judice these last few days!' Nicolas Bentley's cartoon in the* Daily Mail, *3 November 1960.*

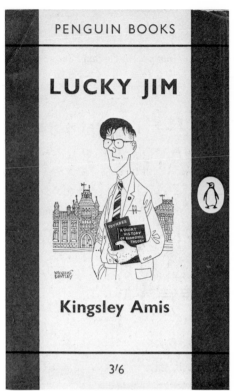

(Above) *Penguin Modern Playwrights, launched in 1966, included Michael Hastings's* Lee Harvey Oswald, *Dennis Potter's* The Nigel Barton Plays *and Peter Terson's* Zigger Zagger.

(Above) *When Kingsley Amis's first novel,* Lucky Jim, *appeared in 1954, it helped to establish the 'anti-hero' of post-war European literature. It was published in Penguin in 1961.*

editorial and managing director, and to rely on a man twenty years his junior, whom he had appointed in May 1960. Tony Godwin had made a reputation as an unconventional bookseller, but his originality and energy

convinced Allen Lane that he should head the editorial team of young men and women Penguin had started to employ in the late 1950s. The firm may have overlooked the work of the 'angry young men' of the mid-1950s, but it soon caught up from 1959 onwards when John Braine's *Room at the Top* appeared, followed in 1960 by John Wain's *Hurry On Down*, in 1961 by Kingsley Amis's *Lucky Jim*, and between 1959 and 1963 by the first seven volumes of the New English Dramatists series, which included writing by Doris Lessing, Arnold Wesker, John Osborne, Anthony Creighton, John Arden, Harold Pinter, Peter Shaffer and Michael Hastings. It was Godwin and his editors who were destined to imbue the Penguin list with the youthful spirit of the 1960s.

(Above) *Iris Murdoch's novel* A Severed Head, *published in 1963, raced into Penguin's bestseller list.*

(Above, right) *Godwin's faith in Harper Lee's* To Kill a Mockingbird *was justified when, after failing to make its mark in hardback, it sold over 200,000 copies as soon as it appeared in Penguin.*

Shortly after taking over the job, Godwin wrote:

The literary scene is in peril of being converted into a dustbowl. At the moment paperback publishers are cashing in on the past 60 years of creative writing and publishing. Unless they take over some of the responsibilities.for discovering and encouraging new talent, the present literary scene will be denuded within the next decade. (New Statesman, 14 July 1961)

He proceeded to divide the Penguin fiction list into easily identifiable series. Penguin Modern Classics, with their grey spines and evocative pictorial covers, gave prominence to mainstream twentieth-century authors such as Joseph Conrad, Ernest Hemingway and Henry James, and to such maverick figures as Isak Dinesen, Oscar Lewis, Wyndham Lewis and Fr. Rolfe. The traditional 'orange' list continued to represent general fiction, including the work of such disparate writers as Anthony Burgess, J. P. Donleavy, Kingsley Amis, Edna O'Brien, Muriel Spark, Penelope Mortimer, Nadine Gordimer, Günter Grass, Iris Murdoch, Margaret Drabble, Saul Bellow, Bernard Malamud, Truman Capote, John Updike, Angus Wilson and John Le Carré.

By 1961, seventy-five million paperbacks were being produced a year in Britain, fifty million of which were sold in Britain. Penguin was competing for authors and titles with about forty other publishers, nine of whom, including Penguin, controlled about 85 per cent of all paperbacks sold. The fiercest rivalry, however, was taking place in bookshops, newsagents and station bookstalls, where Penguin's tastefully designed volumes were battling against other firms' 'breast-sellers'.

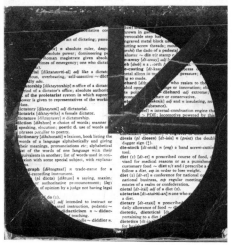

THE PENGUIN ENGLISH DICTIONARY

G.N.Garmonsway

12/6

Wayland Young

The Profumo Affair

2/6
a Penguin Special

Aspects of Conservatism

Godwin retaliated by encouraging new marketing techniques, starting with full-colour covers so that the books could be displayed 'face-forward', followed up by more aggressive advertising, and a push to sell Penguins, as in the early days, in places other than bookshops, such as the recently introduced supermarkets and airport lounges.

He imaginatively expanded Penguin's publishing to include 'egghead' Peregrines, starting with F. R. Leavis's *The Common Pursuit* and William Empson's *Seven Types of Ambiguity*, and moving over into Peregrine some classic early Pelican titles such as *The Waning of the Middle Ages* by J. Huizinga.

At one stroke, ten promising young writers became Penguin authors in January 1962; they included Stan Barstow, Malcolm Bradbury, David Storey and Laurie Lee.

More poetry successfully emerged with the Penguin Modern Poets series. They sold an estimated half a million copies by 1969, with *The New Poetry*, edited by A. Alvarez, reaching Britain's bookshop lists of top ten bestsellers in

(Above. left) *The first* Penguin English Dictionary *sold over a quarter of a million copies within a year of its publication in* 1965.

(Above) *In addition to long-term publishing, there was a return to fast production of Specials of immediate interest, such as* The Profumo Affair: Aspects of Conservatism (1963).

1962, a practically unheard-of achievement for poetry.

Pre-twentieth-century English-language 'classics' were reissued under the series title Penguin English Library so as to include in each volume instructive introductions for 'today's readers'. The West African series metamorphosed, under Ronald Segal's editorship, into the Penguin African Library in response to South Africa's departure from the Commonwealth and the ever-increasing number of newly independent African states (the first twenty-two titles sold in excess of 750,000 copies between 1962 and 1969).

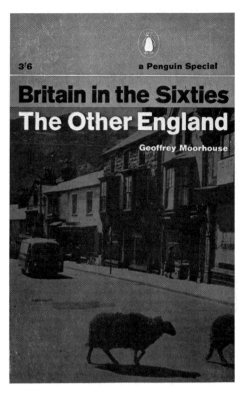

(Above) *McLuhan and Fiore's* The Medium is the Massage (*1967*) *acquired a cult following in the youth culture of the 1960s. Twenty years later, it is almost a metaphor for the decade.*

(Above, right) *A group of books within the revitalized Specials series called* Britain in the Sixties *included* The Other England (*1964*). *Its popularity was so great that it is credited with assisting the defeat of the Conservative Government in 1964. Penguin Inc. followed by commissioning from Michael Harrington* The Other America. *This book on poverty became the number one bestseller there.*

(Opposite page, top left) French Revolution 1968 *by Seale and McConville assessed events in Paris of May 1968. It was published as a Penguin Special in September of that year.*

Pelican, too, took on a new lease of life, its 'backlist' more than doubling between 1960 and 1968 with titles that were not merely topical in the 'swinging sixties' but which have come to represent the essence of the age: J. K. Galbraith's *The Affluent Society*, Anthony Storr's *Sexual Deviation*, R. D. Laing's *The Divided Self*, Vance Packard's *The Hidden Persuaders*, George Steiner's *Language and Silence* and so on.

The Specials series, which had been practically dormant since 1950, woke up again with a What's Wrong with Britain collection, examining national institutions like the church, unions, industry, parliament and hospitals. Other Specials analysed international dilemmas that the post-war generation was now conscious of: *Berlin: Hostage for the West* by John Mander, *Vietnam! Vietnam!* by Felix Greene, *Israel and the Arabs* by Maxime Rodinson and *The Biafra Story* by Frederick Forsyth.

As Penguins multiplied, so Puffins did too. In her first five years with Penguin, Kaye Webb increased the number of Puffins published by

a Penguin Special
in association with Heinemann

French Revolution 1968

With sixteen pages of illustrations

Patrick Seale and Maureen McConville

CENSORED

Sir Allen orders the Puffin Club to drop

psychedelic

(Above) *Kaye Webb's ability to entice young readers to identify with Puffin led to many slogans beginning with P. One London schoolboy suggested 'It's a P'Super – It's a Psychedelic'. When she discovered that the word came from 'the hipster [sic] world of drugs' the slogan was not pursued (Daily Mail, 27 February 1967).*

(Below) *Jill McDonald's drawings of Fat Puffin led to a 'Fat Puffin Loves You' sticker, at the height of the badge craze in 1970.*

50 per cent and increased sales by 300 per cent, with titles like *Mary Poppins* (1962) by P. L. Travers, *The Hundred and One Dalmatians* (1961) by Dodie Smith and *A Bear Called Paddington* (1962) by Michael Bond. Two of her former colleagues said of her: '[She] changed the face of children's publishing in this country'; '[she] had a wonderful capacity for talent spotting in both authors and editors, and a great gift for publicity combined with a strong commercial sense' (*Bookseller*, 2 March 1985).

Her commitment to making reading exciting for children led to the forming of the Puffin Club in 1967. By 1972, one hundred thousand Puffineers had been enrolled – all eagerly awaiting the regular arrival of *Puffin Post*, a magazine devised to market Puffins without selling directly to readers. As well as making reading fun, the Club organized picnics, concerts, holidays, pageants, exhibitions, theatre visits, competitions, parties and even a Think-In at which teenagers were invited to express their views on the kind of reading they would like made available in a

(Below) *Over a million copies of* The Very Hungry Caterpillar *by Eric Carle (1974) are now in print.*

THE VERY HUNGRY CATERPILLAR

by Eric Carle

new imprint called Peacock. Publishing for adolescents has traditionally been a difficult and neglected area. Peacocks attempted to bridge the gap between children's and adult reading. Unfortunately, the series suffered from the fact that the category of adolescent publishing was a new one and therefore book-

(Above) *In 1919 Allen Lane started his career at The Bodley Head offices in Vigo Street, London. Nearly fifty years later he acquired the same premises for his hardback publishing house, Allen Lane The Penguin Press.*

(Above) *The Allen Lane The Penguin Press logo was designed by Hans Schleger.*

sellers had no recognized place in which to display it.

Kaye Webb's zeal for expounding the joys of reading to children was equalled by her ability to publish books to capture their imagination: *A Dog So Small* by Philippa Pearce (1964), *Gobbolino, the Witch's Cat* by Ursula M. Williams (1965), *Comet in Moominland* by Tove Jansson (1967), *By the Shores of Silver Lake* by Laura Ingalls Wilder (1967), *A Wizard of Earthsea* by Ursula Le Guin (1971), *Charlie and the Chocolate Factory* by Roald Dahl (1973), and that book which hooked adults as well, *Watership Down* by Richard Adams (1973). During her twenty years with Puffin, Kaye Webb published over 700 books, a good number of them originals, making it the dominant children's paperback imprint.

'A BOOK IS NOT A TIN OF BEANS'
(Allen Lane quoted in the *Daily Express*, 8 May 1967)

In the spring of 1967 Penguin started a hardback imprint under the name of Allen Lane The Penguin Press.

The biggest slice of my life has been spent in what has been called the 'paperback revolution', and in this latest venture I return to the conventional form of publishing which my uncle John Lane practised when he took me on as a publisher's representative straight from school in 1919. ('A Personal Note' by Allen Lane in the first Allen Lane The Penguin Press catalogue, Spring 1967)

This 'latest venture' was not just a sentimental journey back to conventional publishing, but a move towards consolidating Penguin's position in the paperback world. As established publishers began increasingly to issue their author's works both in hardback and in paperback, so Penguin experienced difficulty in renewing contracts with authors it had traditionally published only in paperback. The solution was to offer authors the opportunity of appearing under one imprint, starting in hardback and, if desirable, moving twelve months later into paperback. Launching the new imprint involved taking a number of risks, and considerable skill was needed. The last thing Allen Lane wanted was to alienate other hardback publishers, on whom Penguin depended for paperback rights, and yet, to be a

(Above) *Ronald Blythe's innovative social documentary account of modern rural life was first published in 1969 by Allen Lane The Penguin Press. It won the W. H. Heinemann Award of the Royal Society of Literature in that year, and went into paperback with Penguin in 1972.*

(Above) *Conversely, Stuart Schram's biography of the leader of the Chinese People's Republic, Mao Tse-tung, appeared first as a Pelican paperback in 1966 and the following year, to give it a more permanent life in college and university libraries, it was published in hardback by Allen Lane The Penguin Press.*

success, Allen Lane The Penguin Press had to be seen as more than just the hardback arm of a successful paperback house.

The first sixteen titles were an eclectic choice ranging from John Berger and Jean Mohr's *A Fortunate Man*, a portrait in words and pictures of an intensely committed doctor working in the remote countryside, to the Mexican poet Octavio Paz's *The Labyrinth of Solitude*, Jules Feiffer's *The Great Comic Book Heroes*, including Superman and Batman, Captain Marvel and Wonder Woman, and Nilsson, Ingelman-Sundberg and Wirsén's *The Everyday Miracle*, a photographic account of life in the womb until birth. Despite many excellent titles, Allen Lane

The Penguin Press always seemed to be over-shadowed by Penguin, and was to experience many difficult years during its search for a hardcover pedigree.

The launching of Allen Lane The Penguin Press was, however, dominated by events within Penguin. Tony Godwin's new team of editors, art directors and marketing staff had together revitalized the look of the books and the manner in which they were sold, giving Tony Godwin the reputation of a man who had *changed the face of Penguin in six years. He brought Penguin into the middle of the twentieth century. He established a vital connection between the editorial and the sales department . . . Godwin*

(Above) *When poor sales figures forced Pan Books to drop Saul Bellow's* Henderson the Rain King, *Penguin leapt at the opportunity to publish it. In September 1966 six works by this important American author appeared simultaneously, promoted by Godwin's new young marketing team. Unfortunately, the striking cover treatments and over-zealous marketing campaign came in for criticism from both the author and booksellers more familiar with Penguin's dignified image.*

(Above, right) *Alan Aldridge gave Graham Greene's* A Burnt-Out Case *(1963) a cover the author considered tasteless. Anthony Powell and John Masters were equally appalled by their Penguin covers, and had no hesitation in making their feelings plain to Allen Lane.*

is virtually irreplaceable. (Tom Maschler, joint Managing Director of publishers Jonathan Cape, quoted by Robert Jones in *The Times*, 5 May 1967)

But a series of incidents brought Allen Lane out of semi-retirement, regardless of failing health, determined to regain control of the firm. He was disturbed by the direction Penguin was taking and in particular by a number of cover designs that had upset authors, one example of which was a charred skeleton seated in a fire-damaged armchair to illustrate Graham Greene's novel *A Burnt-Out Case*. He regarded as unnecessarily extravagant a promotional stunt for Len Deighton's *Funeral in Berlin* which involved flying seventy-five journalists and wholesalers to Berlin (the publicity generated by the exercise resulted in a massive subscription of 480,000 copies of the book). He was appalled at the publication of Siné's *Massacre*, a book of cartoons obsessed with mutilation, the crucifixion, lavatories and nuns (with an introduction, perversely, by Malcolm Muggeridge).

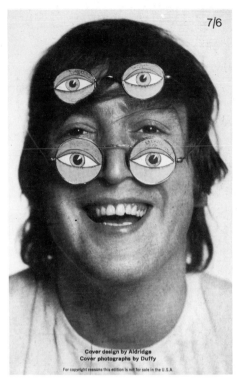

7/6

Cover design by Aldridge
Cover photographs by Duffy
For copyright reasons this edition is not for sale in the U.S.A.

I'm having no more vulgar covers giving a misleading idea about the contents. It's unfair on the public and, besides, our authors should be treated with respect. And there'll be no more gimmicky selling outside proper bookshops . . . Some of the frightful young marketing whizz-kids just wouldn't realize a book is not *a tin of beans.* (Allen Lane interviewed by Anne Batt of the *Daily Express,* 8 May 1967)

In a way that would seem eccentric now, he particularly stressed his dislike of the move to sell paperbacks in supermarkets or chemist shops:

Bookshops today are very different from the kind of forbidding places they were in my youth. When I was a boy, you only expected lawyers, doctors and professors to be seen in them, and there was no question of browsing. That is all quite different now, and I believe they are our best outlets. (Allen Lane interviewed by Willem van der Eyken in the *Financial Times,* 17 March 1967)

After these serious differences of opinion, Tony Godwin left Penguin at the end of April

(Above, left) *Allen Lane's bookselling friends were horrified by* Massacre, *and told him so. His answer to their complaints was to enter the warehouse at dead of night, and, with four accomplices, load every copy on to his farm trailer, drive away and burn them. Next day, the computer recorded the book as 'out of print'.*

(Above) *The excitement and energy of the 1960s were reflected in the youth of the new Penguin team, and in their publishing. John Lennon, poet and most outspoken of the four Beatles, wrote* The Penguin John Lennon, *published in October 1966 – to the glee of his fans and the horror of their parents.*

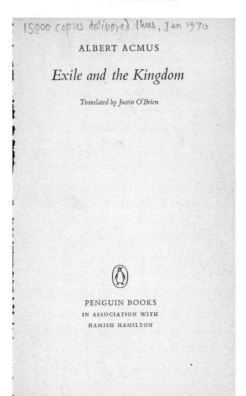

15000 copies delivered thus, Jan 1970

ALBERT ACMUS

Exile and the Kingdom

Translated by Justin O'Brien

PENGUIN BOOKS
IN ASSOCIATION WITH
HAMISH HAMILTON

(Above) *In the order-picking warehouse at Harmondsworth an endless conveyor track propels cartons containing customers' orders to 'picking stations'. The books are packed as the carton steadily moves past. This automation, introduced in 1968, was the first of its kind in British publishing.*

(Left) *Even Penguin can make a mistake. Fifteen thousand copies of Albert Camus's book* Exile and the Kingdom (1970) *were printed with the author's name misspelt.*

1967. On 8 May, Allen Lane issued a statement to the book trade firmly outlining his intentions for the company's future:

Our long-term editorial plans are securely laid and embrace instruction and education in the broadest sense and on a very wide front ... Penguins are deeply committed to distribution through recognized book-trade channels in all their variety ... Future fiction covers will emphasize the Penguin identity (the phrase 'A Penguin Book' is making a prominent return to the front cover). The aim will be visual impact without vulgarity, visual excitement without titillation, clear and legible typography. (Notes for Allen Lane's statement to the *Bookseller*, 8 May 1967)

Godwin's enforced departure was deeply regretted by many of his colleagues. This talented but unpredictable spirit had helped increase the Penguin Group's turnover by nearly 300 per cent in just seven years. He had overseen the doubling of the Pelican backlist and an 83 per cent expansion of the 'orange' Penguin list. He had introduced to Penguin major European writers like Italo Svevo, Jean-Paul Sartre, Albert Camus, Bertolt Brecht, Günter Grass and Isaac Babel. He had taken up the challenge of publishing in paperback works not yet proven in hardback. He had developed the art of fast, polemical publishing with Specials like the Britain in the Sixties library. He had launched the hardback imprint of Allen Lane The Penguin Press, and he had encouraged the development, under Chris Dolley and Charles Clarke, of Penguin Education, which was not just a new series, but a whole division dedicated to publishing books for the decade's rapidly expanding schools and colleges.

In 1967, W. L. Webb, literary editor of the *Guardian*, summed up Penguin as:
more than a business, arguably the most important publishing house in Britain and certainly a national cultural asset whose value can be calculated (worth how many universities, opera houses, art galleries?). (W. L. Webb, *Guardian*, 12 May 1967)

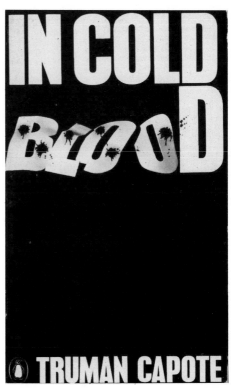

(Above, left) *Sixteen novels by Graham Greene were added in the 1960s to the three published in the 1940s.* The Quiet American (1962), *first published in hardback in 1955, prophetically added another dimension to the USA's involvement in Indo-China.*

(Above) *'We consider books as individual titles, not as categories of Fiction, Whodunits, etc.,' wrote Harry Paroissien, joint Managing Director of Penguin UK, in May 1966. Truman Capote's* In Cold Blood (1967) *is a documentary account of a multiple murder that reads like fiction. Defying classification, it was the forerunner of a number of 'non-fiction novels'.*

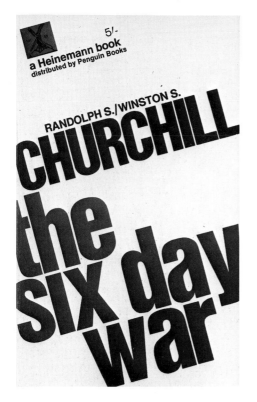

(Above) The Six Day War *by Randolph and Winston Churchill was produced and distributed within six days of the proofs being passed back to the printers, Hazell, Watson and Viney. Allen Lane wrote to Elliott Viney, 'I have been inclined to look back nostalgically at the pre-war years when we used to get a book out in a week, but I do not think that we have ever done better than this' (Letter dated 9 August 1967).*

(Above, right) *Journalist George Perry and Penguin fiction art director Alan Aldridge put together* The Penguin Book of Comics *in 1967. Aldridge's 'pop art' graphics expressed the sense of adventure, optimism and naïvety current among the post-war generation.*

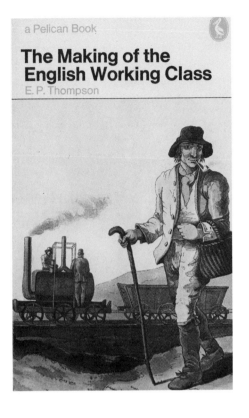

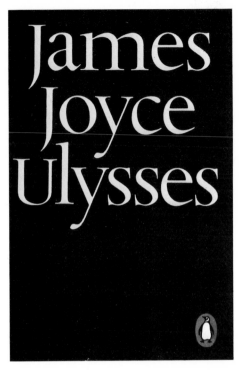

(Above, left) *E. P. Thompson's celebrated book*
The Making of the English Working Class *was
hailed as the greatest and most imaginative post-
war work in English social history when it was
first published in 1963. It became the 1,000th
Pelican in September 1968. To date it has sold
over 180,000 copies.*

(Above) *On 23 April 1969 Allen Lane
celebrated his fifty years in publishing. To mark
the occasion he published in Penguin Joyce's
Ulysses. He himself had secured the rights to
the book for The Bodley Head in 1934, to the
consternation of his fellow directors, because of
the risks of prosecution for obscenity.*

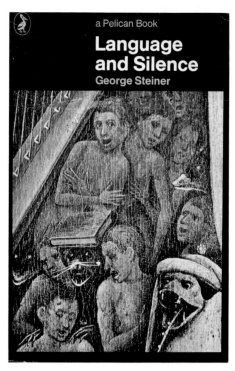

(Above) *Che Guevara's idealism, violence and good looks made him a hero to the youth of the capitalist world even before his death in 1967.* Reminiscences of the Cuban Revolutionary War *and* Guerrilla Warfare *were published posthumously by Penguin in 1969. This poster by Henning Boehlke was produced to promote the books.*

(Above, right) *The 1960s witnessed an upsurge in interest in linguistic philosophy, popularized by the publication in Pelican of Ernest Gellner's* Words and Things *(1968) and George Steiner's* Language and Silence *(1969).*

(Above, left) *Carlos Castaneda's works acquired
a cult following during the peaceful 'hippie' days
of the early 1970s.* The Teachings of Don Juan
was published by Penguin in 1970.

(Above) *Oliver Caldecott, a senior Penguin
editor from 1965 to 1972, recently wrote: 'It
was difficult to persuade my colleagues at
Harmondsworth that . . . a mail order catalogue
offering assorted agricultural implements, heavy
metaphysical tomes and scientific equipment at
dollar prices [was] sensible publishing'*
(Bookseller, 23 March 1985). The Last Whole
Earth Catalog, *put together by the Portola
Institute, California, was published by Penguin
in 1972. It epitomized an approach to
environmental issues that was to gain
respectability by the end of the decade.*

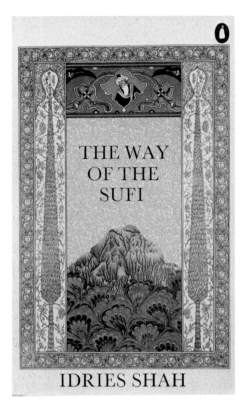

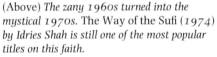

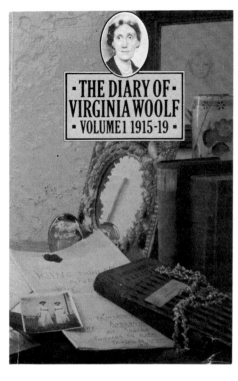

(Above) *The zany 1960s turned into the mystical 1970s. The Way of the Sufi (1974) by Idries Shah is still one of the most popular titles on this faith.*

(Above, right) *The 1970s witnessed a remarkable popular revival of interest in 'Bloomsbury'. It was enhanced by the publication in paperback of* The Diary of Virginia Woolf.

1970–85

'Allen Lane . . . should be regarded as the greatest educative communicator of our time . . . whose contribution to the printed word has never been surpassed.'*

Allen Lane died on 7 July 1970. The next day Penguin announced it was to be taken over by the British business group, Pearson Longman.

Penguin had become a public company in April 1961 when, to raise much needed capital, 750,000 ordinary shares were offered for sale. The offer was 150 times oversubscribed, setting a record for the London Stock Exchange. As the chief shareholder and Chairman of Penguin Books, Allen Lane had been preoccupied for a number of years about the future of the company in the event of his death: would Penguin remain loyal to the aims of popular education?

Penguin had been spending heavily on the new imprint, Penguin Education, since its inception in the summer of 1966. The hardback imprint, Allen Lane The Penguin Press, had yet to make a profit. Competition between rival paperback houses had dramatically increased the sums advanced to popular authors; and rising royalty and discount rates had cut into profit margins. All these factors correspondingly reduced Penguin's profitability, making it vulnerable to takeover, possibly by one of the American firms then investing vigorously in the British market – and, in particular, by McGraw-Hill, which already owned 17.3 per cent of Penguin shares. The announcement that Penguin was to join Pearson Longman was accordingly greeted by the British press with cautious optimism, much emphasis being placed on the complementary nature of Longman's educational commitment to schools and universities.

Bound to be Read, autobiography of Sir Robert Lusty, publisher, Jonathan Cape, 1975.

(Above) *In the summer of 1969 Allen Lane (who had been knighted in 1956) was made a Companion of Honour in the Queen's Birthday Honours List. It was the first time that such a distinction had been bestowed upon a publisher.*

The reduction of profit margins and the hefty investment in editorial enterprises such as Penguin Education and Allen Lane The Penguin Press proved a great burden on resources. Borrowing was increased, but this raised the company's liability on interest payments. However, Penguin was perhaps lulled into a false sense of security, for it was selling more books than ever before. Sales

Penguin to join Cowdray empire

(Above) *Penguin's future after the death of its founder, Allen Lane, was announced in the press on 9 July 1970. The above headline appeared in* the Guardian. *The 'Cowdray empire' is known today as Pearson plc.*

worldwide rose 48 per cent between 1969 and 1974, peaking in that year at forty-four million. Its strategy for overcoming the difficulties was, therefore, not based on classic economic remedies, but on the belief that sales of books from the Penguin backlist, with their better profit margins than new books, would increase by approximately 3 per cent each year. Regrettably, the theory was unfulfilled, and the cash spent on a broad-based effort to market the backlist left little money to promote those new books that had a hope of achieving large sales. These factors unfortunately coincided with the international oil crisis of 1973, bringing in its wake rampant inflation, the three-day working week and a government ban on price increases. All this, combined with the escalating cost of raw materials, severely affected Penguin's cash flow and ability to compete aggressively for continuing rights to works by a number of sought-after authors. There ensued an increasing loss of important twentieth-century writers as hardback publishers such as Heinemann, Chatto and Windus, and Jonathan Cape removed many of their authors' paperback rights from Penguin – the last two forming, with The Bodley Head, a paperback imprint of their own called Triad. This erosion of the famous Penguin backlist came as a serious blow to morale.

The recession then forced the company to look closely at a publishing programme which was continually adding more books to the 4,500 Penguins already available on the 'backlist'. The new chief executive, Peter Calvocoressi, eventually had the painful task of cutting back the number of new titles planned for 1974 from 800 to approximately 540, reasoning,

It's no good having an expansionist policy in a contracting economy. (Peter Calvocoressi,

quoted by Anthony Holden in the *Sunday Times*, 17 March 1974)

One major casualty of the cuts was Penguin Education. Penguin's commitment to education in the broadest sense had been established in 1937 with Pelicans, but books specifically for schools, colleges and universities had started only in 1965 with Hummingbird books for Caribbean schools, sponsored by the Ford Foundation and the University of the West Indies, followed the next year by the Science Teaching Project sponsored by the Nuffield Foundation. *Learning Mathematics*, a course for secondary school students, and *Penguin Modern Psychology*, a series of readings in psychology for university students, appeared in 1966, launching Penguin into the field of secondary and tertiary education.

Penguin Education had developed, by trial and error, a completely new approach to textbook publishing. *Connexions*, a series of 'topic books' for young school leavers and further education students, addressed such subjects as work, marriage, violence and drugs in an exciting magazine format full of photographic illustrations and cartoons with which young people could easily identify. *Voices* was a much praised innovative poetry series for secondary and primary schools.

Penguin Education made an impact because of a freshness of approach and design. They also gave intelligent expression to progressive ideas and developed a personality for their imprint which contrasted usefully with those of their more staid seniors. (*The Times Educational Supplement,* 1 March 1974)

In spite of its enthusiastic devotees, Penguin dissolved the educational division in 1974 and integrated many of its books into Penguin's general publishing. A substantial number of the university-level titles remained in print, but the primary and secondary textbooks, other than those which were economically viable, were dropped and all further investment halted.

Jim Rose, the company's Chairman, and Peter Calvocoressi then had to face head-on the threat posed by other British publishers who were now jacketing their paperbacks more commercially and marketing them more aggressively. The recent losses of rights to works by Ernest Hemingway, Aldous Huxley, James Joyce, Harper Lee, Somerset Maugham,

Iris Murdoch, John Steinbeck, Saint-Exupéry, Virginia Woolf and others collectively amounted to a reduction in sales of over three million books per annum, representing about 10 per cent of Penguin's business throughout Britain and the Commonwealth.

From a worldwide perspective, two factors occurring at roughly the same time spurred Penguin into an important development. On the one hand, Penguin's ability to sell books in the Commonwealth was being reduced by the raid in Britain on paperback rights to authors' works. On the other hand, an investigation in America, which led to the Consent Decree, produced massive concern that British publishers would lose their traditionally exclusive rights to Commonwealth markets. These were both factors in the decision to strengthen the company's presence in America, as it was thought that the United States would be the main beneficiary of a breakdown in territorial rights. If Penguin could not preserve its stake in its traditional markets through London, perhaps the ensuing shortfall could be made up through New York.

In November 1975 Penguin announced its acquisition of a controlling interest in the well-known New York hardback publishing house The Viking Press. The purchase of Viking gave Penguin a distinguished American base and many new copyrights which, for the time being, had to remain within America and the 'open market' (i.e. everywhere except Britain and its Commonwealth countries), but which might eventually be of use within the Commonwealth. Even if the feared breakdown of territorial rights were not to occur, at least the Penguin international grouping acquired the rights to a number of works it had just lost in Britain, including those by James Joyce, Iris Murdoch, Somerset Maugham and John Steinbeck. The Penguin Group could now boast a combined 'backlist' throughout the world of over 8,000 titles. The joint Viking Press and Penguin Books statement to the book trade baldly summed up the move:

Penguin and Viking recognize that the forum for English language publishing is not the United Kingdom or the USA, but the English-speaking world. Penguin and Viking have both long recognized . . . that the old rigid distinctions between hardcover publishing and paperback publishing are becoming obsolete. Penguin and Viking know how

(Above) *'Education's a wonderful thing'* (Sunday Times, *12 July 1970). Heath's cartoon illustrated Penguin policy of the early 1970s. But books for the classroom were to become a casualty of cutbacks in 1974.*

(Above) *Penguin's decision to reduce the number of new titles to be published in 1974, and the dismantling of Penguin Education, received a great deal of publicity. Heath's cartoon appeared in* The Times Educational Supplement, *1 March 1974.*

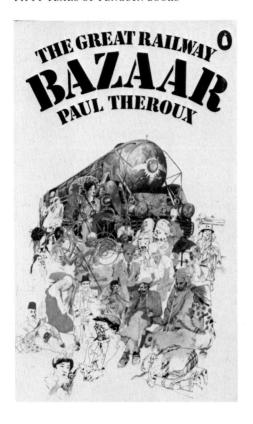

to publish every kind of book, in any appropriate form or shape, in every part of the world. (Viking-Penguin statement printed in the Bookseller, 15 *November* 1975)

'LEFT WING OF THE PENGUIN'
(A headline in the *Daily Telegraph*, 12 April 1977)

Excitement of a different kind erupted when, on 12 April 1977, the *Daily Telegraph* carried an article by Robert Moss accusing Penguin of publishing Marxist-inspired 'agitprop'. The accusation triggered off a succession of letters and articles, culminating in a leader in *The Times* on 21 September headlined 'The Enemies of Liberty'.

Penguin Books, the Open University and many other sources of influence have made not only the jargon but some of the assumptions of socialist analysis familiar, respectable – in some faculties almost obligatory. (The Times, 21 September 1977)

In its defence, Penguin cited many of the obviously non-left-wing books it published: the *Pelican New Testament Commentaries*, the *New English Bible*; the un-Marxist literary autobiographies of Nadezhda Mandelstam, *Hope Against Hope* (1975) and *Hope Abandoned* (1977); and *Progress, Co-existence and Intellectual Freedom* by the courageous Russian dissident, André Sakharov. But Penguin also firmly defended its right to publish 'The Marx Library', Herbert Marcuse, John Berger and the title that started it all, *The Technology of Political Control* by Ackroyd, Margolis, Rosenhead and Shallice.

(Above, left) *Foreign travel has progressively become easier and cheaper with each decade since the war. The dream of 'getting away', and the urgent desire to witness remote places before they are engulfed by technological development, collided in the 1970s, producing some of the best travel writing of this century, such as Paul Theroux's* The Great Railway Bazaar *(1977).*

(Left) *The first page of a three-page announcement on the acquisition of* The Viking Press *in America. It appeared in 'The Organ of the Book Trade', the* Bookseller, *on 15 November 1975.*

The whole episode mirrored Allen Lane's experience in the summer of 1938, when the novelist Ethel Mannin informed him that his association with John Lehmann, Krishna Menon, Ralph Bates and Harold Laski was leading to rumours that he was a member of the Communist Party. Both in 1938 and in 1977 Penguin was quick to refute the allegations of 'Marxist infiltration', and to assert its belief that serious books are of interest to the general public and should, therefore, be made available for general debate. Among the most ambitious of such projects have been the multi-volume Pelican Freud and Marx Libraries.

'FEATHERS FLY AT PENGUIN BOOKS'
(A headline in London's *Evening Standard*,
5 December 1978)

Public debate of Penguin's politics temporarily obscured the more pressing issue of maintaining a large but eroding backlist, an occupation aggravated by problems many businesses were

(Above, left) *Ecology and conservation have become a political cause in the 1980s, thanks to the dedication of a few individuals. Among Penguin authors' works, three have become classics:* Silent Spring *by Rachel Carson (1965),* Ring of Bright Water *by Gavin Maxwell (1974) and* The Worm Forgives the Plough *by John Stewart Collis (1975).*

(Above) *'Lateral thinking' became a popular catch phrase shortly after Edward de Bono's* The Use of Lateral Thinking *was published by Penguin in 1971. By 1985, a total of seventeen works by the author had appeared in Penguin.*

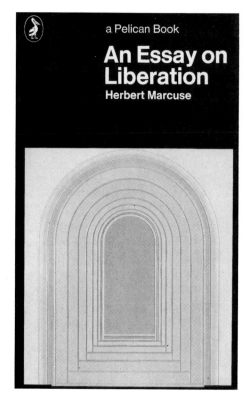

(Above) *John Berger's innovative approach through 'photo-essays' gave great force to his thesis that consumer advertising uses many of the traditions of oil painting.* Ways of Seeing (1972), *produced to coincide with Berger's B B C Television series, quickly became a bestseller.*

(Above, right) *Herbert Marcuse 'suggests that we have discovered the means to undermine western capitalism', ran the blurb on the cover of* An Essay on Liberation (1972) *– a statement guaranteed to upset the 'establishment' during the darkest days of the recession.*

facing in the late 1970s: 'over-manning, over-stocking and over-trading', as the *Bookseller* later described it.

The financial journalist Paul Norkett analysed Penguin's predicament:

There is no disputing Penguin's fine publishing achievements, but in the harsh economic realities of 20 per cent inflation, 18 per cent minimum lending rate, cutbacks in public expenditure, strong sterling, an impending world recession, tough competition and militant trade unions, the management have a difficult task to return Penguin to its former glory. (Bookseller, 14 June 1980)

That Penguin in Britain was in trouble was clear to Peter Mayer when he took up the post of Chief Executive in November 1978. As a successful American paperback publisher, much faith was placed in his ability to restore the company's morale and profitability. He began by challenging Penguin's built-in assumptions and conventions, in an attempt to shake the firm out of complacent attitudes acquired during its days as Britain's unrivalled paperback house. He argued that Penguin's

The Pelican Latin American Library
Carlos Marighela
FOR THE LIBERATION OF BRAZIL

Nadezhda
Mandelstam
'None, not even Solzhenitsyn, has written better'
– Doris Lessing
Hope Against Hope

reliance on a large backlist of titles, and low numbers of books returned unsold from booksellers, was a mixed blessing. The all-important 'backlist' had to be continually replenished by an exciting 'frontlist', and the low 'returns' were probably a result of under-distribution and poor sales. Risks had to be taken.

One of his first actions was to relocate the editorial, art, production and marketing departments, along with the head of sales, under one roof in central London. Editors and art directors had been increasingly operating from London over the previous ten years, but this move in 1979 integrated four publishing activities that Mayer felt could not operate in isolation.

The marketing department was restructured by Patrick Wright, who separated the functions of publicity and promotions. To the consternation of many, Mayer requested full-scale promotions, with targeted sales, of potentially bestselling titles, such as M. M. Kaye's romantic novel, *The Far Pavilions* (1979), the imaginative first novel by William

(Above, left) *The implied allegation of subversive publishing is perhaps more understandable in the case of Carlos Marighela's* For the Liberation of Brazil *(1971). This 'urban guerrilla's manual' contains advice on methods of armed attack and encourages home bomb-making. It transpired that public demand was limited for such a paperback, and the economics of publishing dictated that it went out of print in 1977.*

(Above) *Nadezhda Mandelstam's remarkable autobiography about her early life in Russia is a literary work of great control, force and beauty.* Hope Against Hope *was published in Penguin in 1975.*

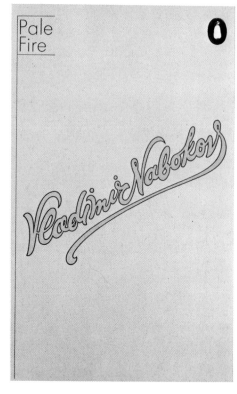

(Above) *Alexander Solzhenitsyn's* One Day in the Life of Ivan Denisovich *was first published in Penguin in 1963. A further seven of his works appeared during the 1970s, helping to make him one of the decade's most famous authors.*

(Above, right) *A Russian of a completely different complexion, Vladimir Nabokov, had nine titles added in the 1970s to the three already available, including* Pale Fire *(1973) and* Bend Sinister *(1974).*

Wharton, *Birdy* (1980), and the thriller/caper by Stephen Sheppard, *The Four Hundred* (1980). This was risk-taking of a new kind for Penguin, and of these first three titles only *The Far Pavilions* was a commercial success.

Jonathan Yglesias's art and production departments were also involved in the re-vamping of Penguin. Existing cover designs were re-examined, resulting in, for example, Graham Greene's *The Human Factor* receiving a four-colour instead of two-colour cover, and more contrasting graphics.

But the most innovative step to be taken was the breaking away for many books from the traditional small 'A' format (181 × 111 mm) Penguin to a larger 'B' format (198 × 129 mm) book, with its correspondingly higher price. Peregrine had begun this trend, indicating that increased prices on a larger format allowed Penguin to publish books that might otherwise be uneconomic.

This move away from the rigid uniformity of the traditional Penguin size and cover price not only added to the company's revenue, but encouraged a more flexible approach to the format of Penguins in general. Under normal circumstances, a Penguin reprint of a work already published in hardback would have been re-typeset to conform to Penguin design standards. But, for many serious books, this observance of house-style was a drain on already limited resources, and often meant that titles would never recover the financial investment made in them. Mayer argued that, had he been presented with the dilemma of wanting to publish the 896-page *Terra Nostra* by Carlos Fuentes, and had he not been able to justify the cost of re-typesetting it, he then would have opted to reproduce the text photographically by offset-litho. He acknowledged that Penguin would thereby have less rigid design standards, but it would acquire an internationally important work for the list without adding uneconomic costs. From 1978 onwards it was no longer necessary for every book to conform to the standard Penguin design and format. This meant that the nature of each work would dictate its presentation. While recognizing the traditional aspect of Penguin design, Mayer realized that the firm's position urgently required flexibility. His goal was to restore the company to its role as a vital publishing force.

During the critical early months of this new policy, the world recession, a strong pound and high interest payments on bank loans made it difficult to attain some of the targets set for Penguin in Britain, and a number of harsh decisions had to be made. The result was a 22 per cent reduction of the new books programme, a ruthless pruning from the 5,000-strong backlist of titles that were selling in insufficient numbers each year, and a cutback of staff by 17 per cent.

As the prominently promoted new books tended to be popular fiction, and a large proportion of the books dropped from the backlist were non-fiction, alarmist speculation led to rumours that Penguin was abandoning its traditional aims and standards.

This overall strategy gives credence to suspicions . . . that while fiction is being strengthened, non-fiction is being further run down, as a continuation of the process that began with the demise of Penguin Education in 1974. ('A Protected Species', Liz Heron, *The Times Educational Supplement*, 29 May 1981)

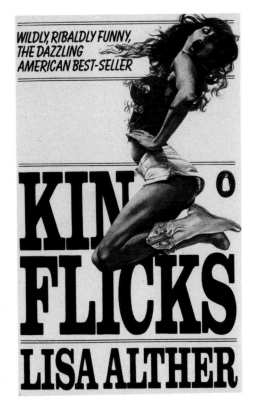

(Above) *Cathy Wyatt's illustration of an all-American cheerleader for the cover and promotional material of Lisa Alther's novel,* Kinflicks *(1977), marked a turning point in Penguin design. Popular fiction would increasingly by given 'popular' cover artwork.*

Penguin's strategy, however, was to supply and maintain a solid backlist of titles through an invigorated and broader new-book publishing programme. Mayer undertook to maintain all the main Penguin series, but in addition he required twelve to twenty-four strong-selling titles each year, many of them quite different from Penguin's recent popular fiction. His intention was to return Penguin in Britain to profitability from a leaner base, and to build up the company again without destroying its traditional image of good value, reliability and range.

The company gradually returned to a creative and expansive style of management

(Above) *Penguin produces an enormous number and range of books by comparison with its rivals in Britain. With finite budgets, individual promotions for every title are impossible. But in 1977 the marketing department came up with an ingenious poster to promote the cookery series.* Know Your Onions *was designed by David Pelham, Penguin's Art Director from 1968 to 1980.*

(Above, right) *In 1983 the entire Pelican Shakespeare series was given a new cover treatment by the distinguished artist/graphic designer Milton Glaser.*

aimed at innovative and lively publishing. Penguins of every shape and size increasingly appeared in the shops: beautifully illustrated, large-format books such as Mark Girouard's social history, *Life in the English Country House* (1980), Raymond Briggs's cautionary tale of life after an atomic explosion, *When the Wind Blows* (1983), the lavish full-colour catalogue to the Tate Gallery's *The Pre-Raphaelites* (1984) exhibition, the very small, cigarette-pack size manual on how to give up smoking, *Stop* (1981), the very fat *Complete Penguin Stereo Record and Cassette Guide* (5th edition 1984), compressing 6,308 entries and reviews into a $2\frac{1}{8}$ inch (55 mm) spine, and the very weighty three volumes of Proust's *Remembrance of Things Past* (1983) in a sturdy slipcase.

Publishing opportunities were quickly snapped up. When the Rubik Cube craze started to become a national obsession, Penguin quickly purchased *Mastering Rubik's Cube* by Don Taylor (1981), and immediately followed it up with an even more successful book. The company's Sales Director, Alan

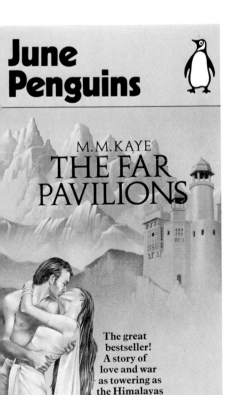

June Penguins

M.M.KAYE
THE FAR PAVILIONS

The great
bestseller!
A story of
love and war
as towering as
the Himalayas

YOU CAN DO THE CUBE

Simple, step-by-step instructions on how
to complete **RUBIK'S CUBE™** by
schoolboy cubemaster **PATRICK BOSSERT**

Wherry, had noted that his neighbour's thirteen-year-old son could solve the puzzle in moments. Puffin offered Patrick Bossert the chance of publishing his secret skill, and later in 1981 *You Can Do the Cube* sold over a million copies in just four months, reaching the top of the children's bestseller lists in Britain and abroad. At the other extreme, in 1980 Penguin published Hofstadter's 'metaphorical fugue', *Gödel, Escher, Bach*, a 778-page tome linking the music of J. S. Bach, the graphic art of Escher and the mathematical theorems of Gödel. Anthony Burgess, reviewing the book in the *Observer*, remarked that 'However little the average reader will understand he is bound to be enlightened on some page or another.' To date, 67,000 readers have taken up the challenge, undaunted by the book's size, complexity and high price.

In October 1980, when seven titles were nominated for the Booker McConnell Prize for Fiction, Penguin secured the rights to five of them within five days. Within a further forty-eight hours, blurbs had been written, covers

(Above, left) The Far Pavilions (*1979*) *by M. M. Kaye was first published in hardback by Allen Lane. In paperback it was given the larger 'B' format size, a price of £2.50 – taking it well past the psychological price barrier of £2.00 – and mass-market promotional material featuring an embracing couple. In six months it sold over 300,000 copies, far outstripping sales of an 'average' Penguin.*

(Above) *Penguins are quite often pirated in India and the Far East, but this is thought to be the first British bootleg Puffin. You Can Do the Cube was found for sale on market stalls in and around London shortly after its publication in 1981. Patrick Bossert, however, received royalties only for the two million copies sold of the real Penguin edition!*

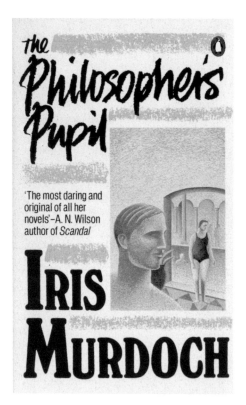

(Above) *After publishing eighteen novels with Penguin in the 1960s and early 1970s, Iris Murdoch was lured away from Penguin for six years. Happily, by 1985, nearly all of her books were once again contracted to Penguin.* The Philosopher's Pupil *appeared in July 1984.*

(Above, right) *'A major artist has once more appeared,' announced the* Spectator *when D. M. Thomas's* The White Hotel *was first published in 1981. This controversial work deals with fantasy and reality in prose and verse, manipulating form to emphasize the content. It appeared as a King Penguin in 1982 and enjoyed a success not usually associated with literary fiction.*

designed and, together with the texts, all despatched to the printers. Within two weeks of the Booker announcement the five new Penguins were on sale in the shops. The speed of the whole operation attracted considerable press coverage for the literary award, and created a genuine sense of teamwork and achievement within the company.

Older members of the book trade were dismayed when, in May 1981, the series name King Penguin was revived and applied to a new, eclectic group of works by among others Angela Carter, Anita Desai, Bernard Mac Laverty, Mervyn Peake, D. M. Thomas, John Kennedy Toole and Patrick White. The books were increased slightly in size to the new 'B' format, and the distinctive orange spine, usually associated with Penguin fiction, was dropped in favour of white. The purpose was to attract greater attention to books that might otherwise have risked being overlooked.

Penguin's policy of publishing across a broad spectrum was continued and extended. The already important area of English Language Teaching for both Europe and the developing countries was augmented with books and tapes, with, for example, *English Right from the Start* by N. and M. Hore (1982) and *Test Your Vocabulary* by Peter Watcyn-Jones (1985). Examination revision aids were published for the first time in 1984 with Penguin Passnotes for O-level, followed in 1985 by Penguin Masterstudies for A-level students.

To expand Penguin's traditional markets, particular titles were selected to appear in a variety of distinctive editions for different age groups and markets. *The Neverending Story* by Michael Ende, for example, is an allegorical tale involving children and fantastical beasts in mysterious places. It appeared in six different guises in 1984: as a King Penguin for the British adult market, as a Puffin for children, as a film tie-in edition to coincide with the release of the film, as an export edition for overseas markets and as two different American editions. The view that a paperback was one edition in one format was finally disproved.

Puffin, first with Tony Lacey and more recently under Liz Attenborough, compounded its earlier successes by adding to its children's list books of an entirely different nature. Fighting Fantasy and adventure gamebooks, referred to as 'inter-active' and 'role-playing' books, require the reader to make choices affecting the outcome of the 'story'. Inspired by the famous American Dungeons and Dragons, Fighting Fantasy has been developed by Ian Livingstone and Steve Jackson to such a degree

(Above, right) Way Ahead *(1985) is a new course in English Language Teaching which provides a course book, a teacher's book, a workbook and a cassette. It complements other similar ELT material, notably the immensely popular* Success with English *series, launched by Penguin Education in 1968.*

(Right) *Penguin Passnotes, begun in 1984, rapidly became market leaders, setting a new standard in quality for revision aids. Over a quarter of a million copies were sold in the first year.*

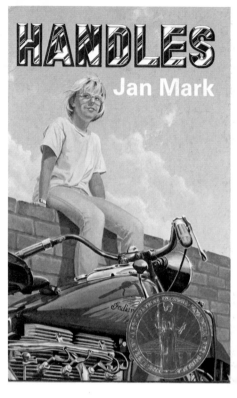

(Above) *Fighting Fantasy is credited with introducing to books some children who would, in other circumstances, completely resist reading. Some of the books are accompanied by software for home computers, turning the 'gamebook' into an elaborate computer game. 'What remains to be a riddle is why highly modern technology and technique should come in shapes from ancient mysteries and the most obscure depths of history'* (The Times Literary Supplement, 25 November 1983).

(Above, right) *Handles, by Jan Mark, won the Library Association's Carnegie Medal in 1984. The care given to Viking Kestrel, the children's hardcover imprint, has earned it over thirty awards in the past fifteen years. The most recent was for* Peepo! *by Janet and Allan Ahlberg.*

(Opposite page, top left) *Before Super Gran became a TV star she looked more like this. Forrest Wilson's eccentric granny has been a popular children's character in Puffin since 1980.*

that they have almost a cult following among children. Since its introduction to shops in 1983, the series has sold over three million books worldwide.

The 'inter-active' theme has even been extended to Puffin Picture Books for the very young so that the child can lift up flaps to discover *Where's Spot* (Eric Hill, 1983), or peek through holes to play *Peepo!* (Janet and Allan Ahlberg, 1983). A new series for teenage children called Puffin Plus was launched in 1980. As well as trying, once again, to create in Britain a recognized category of books for adolescents, its intention is to attract more boys to reading – something they often consider a girl's occupation. The new titles include Jean Ure's *A Proper Little Nooryeff* (1983), about a boy who discovers there is more to ballet than propping up a girl in a tutu, Ursula Le Guin's *A Very Long Way from Anywhere Else*, which portrays a boy's inhibitions about coming to terms with a particular relationship and the teenage

Forrest Wilson

SUPER GRAN

RULES OK!

A
PUFFIN
ORIGINAL

SEE SUPER GRAN ON ITV

during the war but wound down in the mid-1950s, was re-started in 1973. New Zealand, the country with more bookshops per head of the population than any other in the world, had been importing Penguins through agents since before the war, but in 1973 Penguin New Zealand was formed. Both these companies, like the long-established and immensely successful Penguin Australia, not only import, but now publish books for their own markets and the rest of the world. Along with Viking Penguin in America, the Penguin Group will publish over 1,200 new books in 1985, at least one third of which are 'originals' appearing in print for the first time. In addition, Penguin UK will reprint or reissue over 2,500 titles from the backlist.

The growth of Penguin's publishing throughout the group required more co-

(Below) *The Puffin Club publishes two quarterly magazines:* The Egg *for children of four to eight and* Puffin Post *for those of eight to thirteen. Each spring it holds an exhibition-cum-carnival in London for the Club's thousands of members.*

media's insistence on sex, and Anita Desai's *The Village by the Sea*, which describes the problems of two teenagers faced with an out-of-work drunken father, a seriously ill mother and two small sisters too young to understand or help. These contemporary subjects, all treated with a compelling directness, admirably complement perennially popular titles such as *The Scarlet Pimpernel*, *Dr Jekyll and Mr Hyde*, *The Three Musketeers* and *Treasure Island*, which are now published as Puffin Classics.

The Puffin Club has gradually developed into more of a book club for children, and, together with the Puffin Federation which services schools, they have helped to secure for Puffin in 1985 perhaps as much as 40 per cent of the children's paperback market.

PENGUIN IN 1985

These new directions at Penguin in Britain have been reflected throughout the Penguin Group. Penguin Canada, originally founded

Come to
PUFFIN CARNIVAL

Chelsea Town Hall, King's Road, London SW3
7 - 13 April (inclusive) · 10.30 am to 5.00 pm
Admission £1 - Puffin Club Members FREE!

Fairground Sideshows · Computer Arcade
Fun House · Spooky Book Walk
Films · and lots more
Plus your favourite authors and illustrators
Opening Ceremony by ROALD DAHL - 7 April

(Below) *The Ron Blass warehouse, completed in March 1985, was named after Penguin's Vice-Chairman who died unexpectedly in November 1984. Ron Blass joined the company in 1942 and, after four years in the Royal Navy, returned as a company van driver. His innate business sense ensured fast promotion through the sales department, and in the late 1960s led to his spearheading the complete modernization of Penguin's warehousing and distribution systems. This new extension to the warehouse at Harmondsworth now gives Penguin the capacity to store over forty million books.*

(Above) *Audrey Eyton's* F-Plan Diet *has been translated into sixteen languages and worldwide sales are over three million. Its huge success is exemplified by New Zealand. 'The F-Plan [high fibre] diet book sold 75,000 copies in forty-nine days . . . at the current rate of sales it will take only one year eight months and two weeks to have sold one copy of* The F-Plan *for every one of the one million households in the country'* (New Zealand Publishing News, *November 1982*).

ordination as books increasingly raced in every direction around the world. This has led to an expansion of John Rolfe's print control department which, as well as overseeing production and publishing programmes of the rapidly expanding British list, also manages efficient levels of stock at the Harmondsworth warehouse.

The all-important decision of what to publish in Britain rests with Editorial Director Peter Carson who, with Tony Lacey, Viking Editorial Director, and Fanny Blake, Penguin Fiction Editor, heads a team of twelve commissioning editors for the adult hardback and paperback lists. Puffin and Viking Kestrel are in the charge of Liz Attenborough and Sally Floyer. The critical calculation of price, print quantity and format for each book is made by the editorial department and print control, while at another weekly meeting, chaired by Art Director Steve Kent, views are expressed from different departments on the vital question of cover designs for every one of the books in the enormous Penguin list.

(Right) *The potential for joint printings and for international marketing and exchange of stock led to the worldwide use in 1984 of the long-established Viking imprint for hardbacks, to parallel Penguin for paperbacks. The children's hardbacks were also re-named Viking Kestrel.*

Recent advances in printing technology greatly assist Penguin's policy of re-assessing each aspect of every one of the 6,000 titles in the backlist. Only a few years ago, low sales figures would have indicated that certain books be dropped from the list. But today, unlike almost any other paperback publisher, Penguin is prepared to make financial sense of books that might sell as few as 1,000 copies a year – excellent titles such as Sir John Summerson's *Georgian London* under the Peregrine imprint, and others with a strictly limited market, such as *Jewish Poets of Spain* or Claude Lévi-Strauss's *Structural Anthropology*.

With the company's renewed ability to publish a few especially strong-selling novels like Shirley Conran's *Lace* and Stephen King and Peter Straub's *The Talisman*, Penguin is once again catering for practically every section of the market throughout the world. The list ranges from William Lorimer's *The New Testament in Scots*, Tom Hadden and Kevin Boyle's Penguin Special *Ireland: A Positive Proposal*, and the forthcoming Pelican, *Hanes Cymru* (a history of Wales in Welsh), to M. J. Akbar's *India: The Siege Within* and Gough Whitlam's *The Whitlam Government*; from Richardson's *Clarissa* and Dostoevsky's little-known first novel, *Netochka Nezvanova*, to Geoffrey Hill's *Collected Poems* and Yukio Mishima's extraordinary *The Sea of Fertility* tetralogy. Fine novelists first published by other companies in the Penguin Group, such as William Kennedy (USA), Robertson Davies (Canada), David Malouf (Australia) and Frank Sargeson (New Zealand), are published in Britain. There is new thinking in history, politics and economics – the 1985 list includes Jane Jacobs, Milton Friedman, Edward Said, Martin Wiener and Shirley Williams. There is *Beyond Ultimate Trivia* and Roald Dahl's *BFG*, Beatrix Potter's *Derwentwater Sketchbook* and Betty Root's educationally innovative *Step*

(Below) *As a result of Pearson's purchase of Penguin in 1970, Longman Young Books for children were transferred to Penguin and became the hardback imprint Kestrel. Leon Garfield's popular stories for children now appear in both Viking Kestrel and Puffin.*

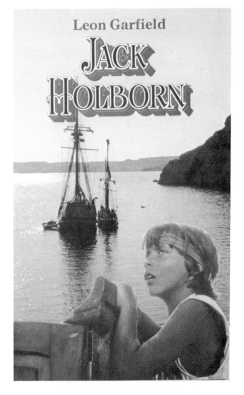

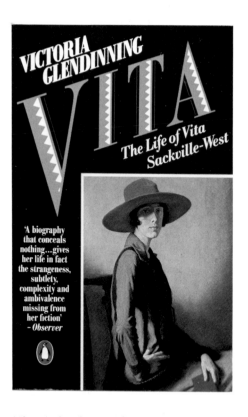

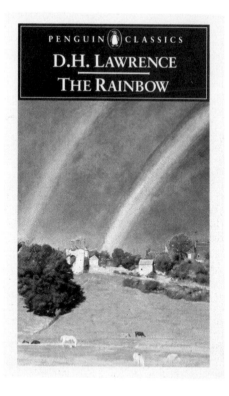

(Above) *The advance in literary techniques and the expansion of subject matter to include the whole range of human experience has greatly benefited the art of biography.* A. J. A. Symons's The Quest for Corvo (*1940*), Hesketh Pearson's The Life of Oscar Wilde (*1960*), *Michael Holroyd's* Lytton Strachey: A Biography (*1971*) *and Victoria Glendinning's* Vita: The Life of Vita Sackville-West (*1984*), *all help to substantiate Robert Gittings's claim that 'These fifty years have been a golden age of biography'* (The Nature of Biography, *Robert Gittings, 1978*).

(Above, right) *The famous black Penguin Classics series has been broadened in* 1985 *to incorporate English authors, and extended to include works written in the twentieth century. The series now contains over* 750 *titles, all of which will eventually receive the new style of cover design shown here. The famous black spines remain, but a helpful band of colour at the top indicates the cultural provenance.*

Ahead Workbooks. Penguin's 1985 list includes recent fiction from Richard Adams, Kingsley Amis, Saul Bellow, Dirk Bogarde, William Boyd, Shirley Conran, Nadine Gordimer, Stephen King, Doris Lessing, David Lodge, John Mortimer, Iris Murdoch, Leslie Thomas and John Updike.

Since 1979, Penguin has evolved a more flexible form of financial management which offers guidelines within which the company can work, but which accommodates the new Penguin philosophy of quick response to opportunities and greater willingness to take risks. Penguin's Finance Director, John Webster, has developed systems which permit imaginative publishing without the imposition of rigid structures.

One feature of the current period is its openness to new ventures of varying sorts, ranging from the increasingly diversified list, the creation and acquisition of copyrights, the growth of hardback publishing (Viking has doubled the number of books in its 1985 programme), to new direct approaches in export markets in Europe, and even a move into bookselling. In 1980 the first Penguin bookshop was opened in Covent Garden, London. John Hitchin now manages a chain of nine shops, stocking not only all Penguin's imprints, but thousands of titles from other publishers too. Penguin's renewed profitability enabled it in July 1983 to purchase the long-established publishing house of Frederick Warne, thus adding to the children's list Beatrix Potter's charming Peter Rabbit books, as well as the myriad of merchandise items developed from her many characters.

In May 1985, Penguin acquired from the International Thomson Organization the well-known publishing houses of Michael Joseph, Hamish Hamilton, Sphere paperbacks and Rainbird, and the warehouse and distribution company TBL Book Service. On announcing the news Peter Mayer said:

Together with Viking and Warne we are instantly among the largest hardcover publishers in the Commonwealth. With Sphere and Rainbird, this acquisition has positive implications for us all over the world. We are certain it will strengthen our [Penguin] group and offer us and our new colleagues additional opportunities. (Penguin press release, 1 April 1985)

As hardback and paperback publishers of books for all ages and tastes, producing books in five countries, selling fifty million copies worldwide, Penguin still maintains that:

Everything starts with the book – authors and ideas. Penguin can't be right unless Penguin publishing is right. (Peter Mayer, interviewed by John Archer for BBC Television, March 1985)

Over the last five years, the company has sought not only to return to profitability, but to prepare itself for the challenges of the future, some of which could not even have been guessed by Allen Lane when he began Penguin in 1935. However, Allen Lane's vision of expanding the habit of reading and of combining change with traditional values remains a guiding force within the company today. Penguin continues to strive 'to supply something for all needs and moods' (*Ten Years of Penguin*, Penguin Books, 1945).

The Tale of Peter Rabbit – *in Welsh.*

(Above) *The first Penguin Bookshop opened in Covent Garden in 1980, followed in quick succession by another eight, the most recent of which is the Puffin Bookshop, also in Covent Garden, which opened on 30 July 1985, the very day of Penguin's fiftieth anniversary.*

A selection of contemporary Penguins shows the range
and diversity of series, subject matter, format and design.

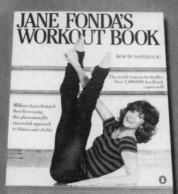

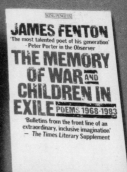

In recent years Penguin has put less stress on a 'Penguin look'
except within coherent series, choosing instead
to emphasize author, title and potential readership.

Jeremy Aynsley

FIFTY YEARS OF PENGUIN DESIGN

Over the last fifty years which mark the history of Penguin Books, the issue of covers and the interior design of paperback books has raised certain important questions. These questions relate to both Penguin and paperback publishing in general. They concern the role of the designer in mass-production and also involve our daily responses to the appearance of books – that is, our tastes. Should what is now an industrial product declare itself as such, or should it evoke its craft origins by its decoration or form?

Inevitably, the process of book design is defined by editorial patterns and redefined by changes in readership, market interests which coincide with these changes, and technological advances. Decisions made in the art and design departments in response to the editorial briefing and marketing requirements are in some ways the most important part of this process, because they aim at securing the market initially and in the long term. It has never been different, even if it is tempting to think that the first Penguin typographical covers were 'natural' or inevitable.

Few subjects in a paperback house generate so much heated discussion as cover designs. Generalizations in the field are particularly risky, yet everybody is eager to express opinions meant to help the art director in his task, or critical of what he submits. The problem is this: a cover design should reflect, or be relevant to, the contents and character of the book; it should appeal to, or intrigue, the potential buyer; it should be recognizable as a family (a group of volumes by the same author, for instance, or a series of books on related subjects); it should be easily identified as coming from a publisher proud of his imprint; in a world of rapidly changing graphic fashions, it should stand out from, or at least stand up to, what is displayed to its left and right, above and below; the author should like it or at any rate not violently object to it; it should be easy to reproduce, and not be exorbitantly expensive to print; and if possible it

should be beautiful or original or witty in its own right. (Hans Schmoller: 'The Paperback Revolution' in *Essays in the History of Publishing,* Longman, 1974, p. 317)

This view accurately reflects the delicate balance required between marketing and design, which has become all the more crucial in the competitive world of paperback selling in 1985. However, since Hans Schmoller's essay was written, the design of the Penguin is no longer governed by the overriding wish to establish the publisher's identity, but rather by the need to find the correct balance to suit individual titles. This is especially the case when books are not part of an identifiable series.

What follows is an account of some of the solutions to those tasks, provided from the range of Penguin's fifty years.

A REPRINT SERIES

Edward Young's design for the first ten covers [C1]* of the newly established reprint series in July 1935 proved to be more than just a sensible response to the demand for cheap, effective layout. The combination of Gill Sans-Serif Bold, broad colour bands and convenient size was to become the formula which Penguin would keep for its fiction titles until the early fifties, and its ghost would haunt even later reforms.

Good typefaces, based on the classical faces of the Renaissance and seventeenth and eighteenth centuries, had been made available for machine composition increasingly during the 1920s by the work of Beatrice Warde and Stanley Morison at the Monotype Corporation. Instilled with the principles of the Arts and Crafts reform movement, which had their earlier impact on the private presses, the revision of old types was complemented by the

* Numbers in square brackets refer to the colour inset.

commission of new faces. In this way Eric Gill had been asked to translate to a typeface Edward Johnston's sign lettering, seen since 1916 on the stations of the London Underground. For the texts, the first Penguins made use of Stanley Morison's Times New Roman of 1931. Therefore, as they appeared in the first series of ten, the books had a happy combination of novelty and familiarity: they evoked something fresh and modern, while not being so rarefied or 'moderne' as to discourage the customer from picking them up.

Richard Hoggart has analysed his initial reaction:

Just why Penguins were able to enlist this degree of enthusiasm – and to command a kind of loyalty – is worth teasing out. They were very cheap of course and attractively presented – they looked neither meretriciously glossy nor ponderously dull. They gave us the chance to own, say, some good contemporary novels and essays . . . whereas before we had been almost confined to secondhand copies of older writers. (Richard Hoggart: 'The Reader', *Penguins Progress 1935–1960*, Penguin Books, 1960, p. 27)

Hoggart isolates the books' cheapness and contemporaneity as two important features which attracted him and would determine their success. They were aspects which the rest of the publishing world had forecast as their potential undoing. However, Allen Lane was convinced that his estimate of the likely market and the quantity of reprints that would be needed was right. Hoggart at this time was a sixteen-year-old grammar school boy in a provincial town. His interest in such a series symbolizes a reaction against Edwardian culture and the stuffiness and insularity in which he had grown up.

For non-fiction, Allen Lane's approach was to commission specialists to write introductory accounts of their subjects, which would guarantee a broad, loyal readership. This policy was initiated when the Pelicans were introduced with Bernard Shaw's commissioned version of *The Intelligent Woman's Guide to Socialism, Capitalism, Sovietism and Fascism*, in two volumes, in May 1937. Allen Lane's 'intelligent layman', a product of the BBC, the Workers' Educational Association and possibly the Left Book Club, was to be the basis of Penguin's growth. Such popular magazines as *Picture Post* and *Lilliput* had also started to open up serious subjects for the lay reader by their photo-essays and articles on current affairs and world events.

The importance of Europe was recognized both in editorial decisions and in the initial design and conception of Penguins. Editorially this acknowledgement was made necessary by the rise in concern about continental Fascism. The early Penguin Specials reflected this: the first title, in November 1937, was *Germany Puts the Clock Back* by Edgar Mowrer [c4], which was followed by G. T. Garratt's *Mussolini's Roman Empire* and *Blackmail or War?* by Geneviève Tabouis (both February 1938). Books written by *émigré* specialists were to become a central feature.

In design also, Allen Lane acknowledged the influence of German reprint series. Many of the characteristics of Penguin's design were already evident in the Albatross series of reprints. Albatross books, themselves based on the Tauchnitz editions of Leipzig started in 1842, were founded in Hamburg in 1932 by J. Holroyd-Reece, Max Christian Wegner and Kurt Enoch. Albatross had been the first to colour-code their series by genre – blue for love stories, green for travel, orange for novels and short stories and so on.[1] The size, $7\frac{1}{8}$ by $4\frac{3}{8}$ ins. (181 by 111 mm), was based on the requirements of standardized production, but also happened to relate approximately to the Golden Section, a feature which was to satisfy designers for Penguin throughout its subsequent developments [c2]. Albatross, like Penguin, had typographical covers with the title in sans-serif capitals and made a feature of their bird colophon. The typographer was Hans (Giovanni) Mardersteig, who produced a well-spaced, evenly toned page, in contrast to Tauchnitz's rather badly crowded page.

At first Penguin books were produced with dust-jackets covering the paperback covers. They also included a description of the author and a small photograph, initially inside on the flap of the dust-jacket, then on the rear cover.

---

1. For an account of the development of other paperback series, in Germany and the United States as well as in Britain, see Piet Schreuders: *Book of Paperbacks*, Virgin Books, London, 1981.

The look of Penguins was partly determined by the facilities the printer could provide and partly by the specifications of the production team. In the early years, design fell into the sphere of production, with Edward Young, Bob Maynard and John Overton, as successive Production Managers, devising layouts and making decisions about typography. The separation of design from production and then cover artwork from typography at Penguin reflected broader changes which acknowledged the growth of the graphic design profession in Britain which was to accelerate after 1945.

Penguin was the overall series title incorporating orange for Fiction, cerise for Travel, dark blue for Biography, green for Crime and Detection, yellow for Miscellaneous, and grey for Current Affairs [c1].

The Penguin Shakespeare series had begun in April 1937, the individually commissioned Penguin and Pelican Specials followed in November, the Illustrated Classics (a short-lived series of ten) were published simultaneously in May 1938, and finally, in March 1939, the Guides, all of which reflected the rapid acceptance of paperback buying. In November of that year another special series on a peculiarly eclectic range of subjects was introduced, known as King Penguins. These were slightly wider in format, bound in boards covered with patterned papers.

With the exception of the King Penguins, the size of all series remained the same as for the original Penguins. The Pelicans began in their characteristic blue, and were not illustrated at the start. The Pelican Special *Modern German Art* (July 1938), written by O. Bihalji-Merin under the pseudonym of Peter Thoene, had sixteen photogravure plates, reproductions of paintings shown the previous year in the Munich Exhibition of Degenerate Art. The Specials stood out from other series for their inclusion of copy in the white panel of the cover. Often red and white to denote their topicality and urgency, their similarity to magazine production in commissioning time was emphasized when new chapters were added to reprints [c4]. Line-drawings printed by letter-press, useful for diagrammatic and statistical information, but also used evoc-

atively as by Gertrude Hermes for the Penguin edition of Izaak Walton's *The Compleat Angler* [c5], were also to become a regular feature of Pelicans.

The intention of the Illustrated Classics was to provide a series which would give readers the quality of illustrated novels obtainable in hardback, but at the same price as regular Penguin fiction. With experience of The Bodley Head behind him, Allen Lane had a model to follow. Not only in book illustration, but also in the pages of magazines such as the *Radio Times* since its start in 1923, there had been a taste for small vignettes, often on scraperboard, linocut or wood-engraved. The Society of Wood-Engravers provided a source of illustrators for Robert Gibbings, the series' Art Editor [c6]. The Society had been formed in 1920, with Eric Gill and John Nash amongst its founder-members, in order to establish the craft of small-scale, detailed wood-engravings, which were most suitable as illustrations to

1. *The Penguin Shakespeare* Twelfth Night, *first edition, designed by Edward Young in* 1937.

ACT ONE

Enter Orsino, Duke of Illyria, Curio, and other Lords
DUKE: If music be the food of Love, play on,
    Give me excess of it: that surfeiting,
    The appetite may sicken, and so die.
    That strain again, it had a dying fall:
    O, it came o'er my ear, like the sweet sound
    That breathes upon a bank of violets;
    Stealing, and giving odour. Enough, no more,
    'Tis not so sweet now, as it was before.
    O spirit of Love, how quick and fresh art thou,
    That notwithstanding thy capacity,
    Receiveth as the sea, nought enters there,
    Of what validity, and pitch soe'er,
    But falls into abatement, and low price
    Even in a minute; so full of shapes is fancy,
    That it alone, is high fantastical.
CURIO: Will you go hunt my Lord?
DUKE: What Curio?
CURIO: The hart.
DUKE: Why so I do, the noblest that I have:
    O when mine eyes did see Olivia first,
    Methought she purg'd the air of pestilence;
    That instant was I turn'd into a hart,
    And my desires like fell and cruel hounds,
    E'er since pursue me. How now what news from her?
    Enter Valentine
VALENTINE: So please my Lord, I might not be admitted,

17

private press book editions, but were to find new contexts in more commercial work in the interwar period.

In spite of being an interesting precedent to the Puffin Story Books and to the use of illustrations in the Handbooks, the Illustrated Classics series was considered unsuccessful. J. P. Morpurgo has commented:

Their extravagant elegance did not match either the bustling, youthful vigour of Penguin or the starkness of a world hurtling towards war. The weaknesses of illustration were exacerbated by the indifferent quality of the paper and by the Penguin format, seemingly too cramped to carry illustrations. (Allen Lane, King Penguin, Hutchinson, 1979)

This points up the inherent restrictions in the traditional paperback format, especially before paper quality improved. By contrast, the Penguin Shakespeare was considered a satisfactory series, even if it reached typographical eloquence only in Jan Tschichold's revisions after 1947. In the first editions the use of the Monotype Times New Roman typeface suited the printing on cheap paper (Figure 1).

KING PENGUINS

King Penguins deserve a section to themselves. Begun at the unlikely time of the outbreak of war and, therefore, prone to the failure which had met the Illustrated Classics, they were in fact highly acclaimed. Again the inspiration had come from Germany. The Insel Verlag at Leipzig had started its Insel Bücherei in 1912.

Elizabeth Senior, brought in from her post at the British Museum, was the first editor of the King Penguins, but after her untimely death in a London air-raid the series was taken over by Nikolaus Pevsner in 1942. An example of her adaptation of Redouté's *Book of Roses* shows how closely it followed the Insel tradition [c7]. With improvements in printing overseen by R. B. Fishenden, the covers became pictorial and the particular difficulties of printing small-scale reproductions were overcome. The subjects of King Penguins ranged from the familiar – a flora, a book of birds, several other natural history subjects, *Ackermann's Oxford* – to more historical subjects such as the *Bayeux Tapestry* and to eccentric titles ideal for illustration such as *Ballooning*. Allen Lane was

immensely proud of the series, introducing them with the following remarks:

The aim of King Penguins is different [from that of Modern Painters]. These have not been planned to coincide with the public's growing appreciation of art, but rather to appeal to the general liking for illustrated keepsakes. For this reason they are specialized . . . One of the most distinctive features of this series is their decorative covers . . . [These were] used very sparingly by the English publishers before the War, but both in our King Penguins and in our Puffin Story Books we have found this not only an attractive manner of decorating the binding of books but also giving the artist a share in book design. (Quoted in David J. Hall, The King Penguin Series, Penguin Collectors' Society, 1980, p. 3)

As Allen Lane made clear, the intention was to offer popular decorative books, and any criticism of their conservatism should take this into account. An example of a more adventurous experimental book is *A Prospect of Wales*, in which the painter Kenneth Rowntree used post-Cubist space for his landscape cover [c8]. The books' general achievement was that, while covering what might be considered minority interests, they were written by experts in these fields and were presented as a series, encouraging collectors to buy them all. An indication of their design standards is their appearance in many of the National Book League awards exhibitions. Jan Tschichold's revision of *A Book of Scripts* [c9], printed in Monotype Bembo as an adaptation of Juan de Yciar's 1547 book and with hand-drawn additions such as the lettering on the cover by Tschichold, was claimed to surpass Insel Verlag at its best.

PUFFIN INTERLUDE

At the same time as King Penguins, another illustrated project was started – Puffin Picture Books. Noel Carrington, working on illustrated books at the Country Life Press, approached Allen Lane with the idea of publishing a series of low-cost children's books. As a father of young boys, he was prompted partly by the dearth of such material and partly by the example of contemporary Soviet and French paperbound books. One of the books Carrington took to persuade Allen Lane was an edition of the Père Castor series.

As long as the price was kept to sixpence and the books could be packed with other Penguins, the series could go ahead. To keep the costs low the books were to be illustrated by autolithography, thereby avoiding the intermediate process of transferring the artist's drawing by a trained lithographer. There was resistance from the unions at a time of job insecurity, but none the less illustrators worked at the printers directly on prepared zinc plates. The books were exactly twice the width of ordinary Penguins, which facilitated packing [C10, C11 and C12], and were usually of horizontal or 'landscape' format and of thirty-two pages, made up of sixteen sheets with integrated colour illustrations and text on one side, black and white on the verso. The initial conception would be prepared on tracing paper, drawn full-size, the colour pages simply in coloured pencil, the text typed on. On acceptance by Carrington, black line-drawings were sent to the printers, W. S. Cowell of Ipswich, who produced lithographic plates. The illustrator then completed the design. At first these plates were the usual zinc, but by 1946 Cowell's had developed plastic plates which allowed the illustrator to work on a lighter material and also showed the colours as they would be when printed on a white page.[2]

The text was occasionally designed by the illustrator, but after Jan Tschichold's arrival it was more often the typographer's task. Print runs were usually 10,000. The range of subjects partly reflected Noel Carrington's children's interests and partly what was considered suitable for a rounded education: nature, history, machines, building, and social geography, but also stories which, at a time of war, introduced children to different national-ities. Children evacuated to the countryside might be helped to adapt with books on country life and the farm.

2. Margaret and Alexander Potter have outlined their work on several of the series: 'The zinc plate reached the illustrator as one piece 38 by 33 ins., a large area to stretch across; for each colour there would be a separate plate, usually blue, red, green and yellow, possibly grey for tone. Occasionally the illustrator would follow a poster-colour dummy. Also a pattern sheet from the printer would help the illustrator to choose the particular tone and strength of lithographic colour most suitable for illustration. The plates, completely litho-chalked, were then returned for printing and in usual fashion attached to an offset machine.'

2. The Family from One End Street *introduced to Puffin as a story book in 1942, with illustrations by the author, Eve Garnett.*

The Puffin Picture Books were such a good blend of editing and design that, with the Puffin Story Books, they formed the basis of many children's reading habits. The Puffin venture would grow increasingly until, by 1985, they made up one third of the annual sales of all Penguin books.

Puffin Picture Books had established a reputation for presenting children's non-fiction in a striking larger format. Gradually the subjects became increasingly orientated towards the classroom and reference material, and the role of providing good literature was taken over by Puffin Story Books. These were in the conventional Penguin size and at the same price. Starting in 1941 under the editor-ship of Eleanor Graham, the first title was Barbara Euphan Todd's *Worzel Gummidge*. At first the age-group of the reader was nine to thirteen, but this soon broadened. As a guide to

3. *Walter Trier's illustrations to the ever-popular* Emil and the Detectives, *which was translated for Puffin in 1959, depended on swift and economic line-drawing.*

4. Alice in Wonderland *was adapted to Puffin format in 1946 with the original Tenniel illustrations.*

the buyer, later covers included a suggested reading age. The policy for the covers was to continue the typographical formula, with red panels, Gill Sans-Serif Bold for titling and a small illustration at the centre. The interiors combined a large body of type with line-drawings. The requirements of letter-press production encouraged atmospheric illustrations in which diverse approaches to figure drawing were shown. An artist's identity was revealed most fully in details such as hatching and overall quality of line. Realism seemed most suitable in those areas of fiction intended for libraries and as books which parents would buy for children (Figures 2 and 3).

To my delight Allen asked one day if I would like Henry Williamson's Tarka the Otter, *adding that we would get good illustrations for it. I had seen it at Bumpus's when it was first published and always had a pile of it in the Children's Room.*

There were beautiful decorations by Tunnicliffe, and again I wrote an introduction to it. (Eleanor Graham, 'The Puffin Years' in Worzel Gummidge, *Penguin Books, 1981)*

In its early days, the Puffin list made children's classics available. Among the first titles were *Alice's Adventures in Wonderland* (Figure 4), using the original John Tenniel illustrations, in 1946, followed by a paperback edition of *Grimm's Fairy Tales* in 1948, *Tarka the Otter* in 1949, *Ballet Shoes*, also in 1949, and *Little Women* in 1953. The covers evolved with full-scale illustrations in 1949: Eleanor Graham and Hans Schmoller favoured the established children's illustrators, such as Edward Ardizzone and David Gentleman, whose work was often incorporated into the covers using a pastel-shaded wash of pink, pale blue or yellow. On other occasions a bolder approach, such as the silhouetted cut-outs

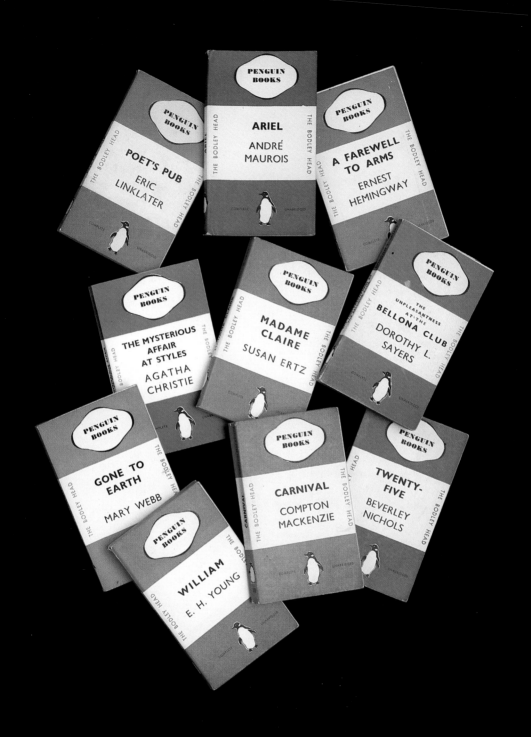

[c1] The first ten books, which appeared in July 1935, established the Penguin formula of strong typographical covers. Edward Young, the designer, used sans-serif and horizontal bands of colour and drew the Penguin colophon. Green bands indicated Crime, orange Fiction and dark blue Biography. Later, grey was introduced for Current Affairs, yellow for Miscellaneous and cerise for Travel.

[c2] The Albatross design, with its sans-serif titling, colour-coding and the bird colophon, had been in use since 1932 and was the basis for the Penguin cover.

[c3] Light blue was used for the non-fiction Pelican. The shade increasingly darkened, until it became the present characteristic turquoise in 1961.

[c4] Inclusion of text helped to evoke the urgency of production when new editions were published incorporating further chapters. For this the tripartite divisions were abandoned.

[c5] An early illustrated cover showing Gertrude Hermes' wood-engraving of 1939. Letterpress line-drawings accompanied the text.

[c6] The use of wood-engraving, under the illustrated Classics Art Editor Robert Gibbings, introduced to a paperback series a style of illustration previously associated with the private presses.

[c7] With the King Penguins colour illustration became integral to the design from the start. Early titles in this series depended on the Insel Verlag formula.

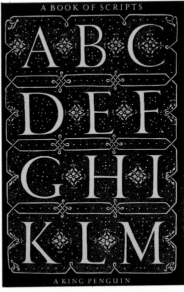

[c8, c9] More adventurous productions for King Penguins were overseen by R. B. Fishenden after 1942.

[C10] PUFFIN PICTURE BOOKS: *Orlando's Evening Out*, a very popular Puffin Picture Book, shows the full use made of the page by Kathleen Hale.

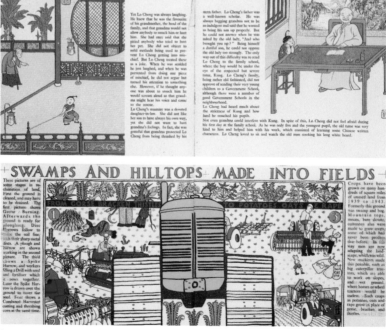

[C11, C12] Experiments in page layout led to imaginative and decorative solutions: *Lo Cheng*, by Chiang Yee (above), and *A History of the Countryside*, by Margaret and Alexander Potter (below).

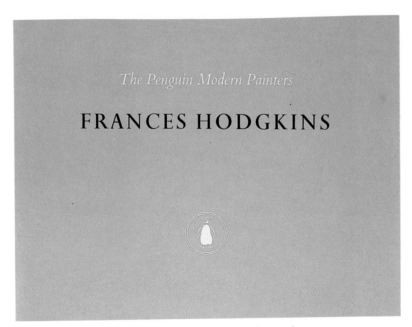

[c13] The Penguin Modern Painters provided sixteen colour and sixteen
black and white horizontal-format illustrations. After 1949 they included a paper
dustjacket and typographical cover designed by Hans Schmoller.

[c14] An experimental cover and page layout was used for larger-format pictorial
books. Their production was overseen by Ruari McLean. They dealt with art, design
and architecture at the time of postwar reconstruction.

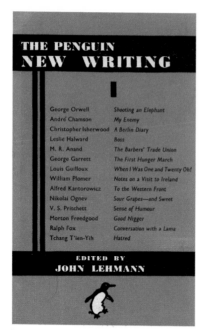

[C15, C16] An early hard-edge approach for The Penguin New Writing series, softened from no. 27 onwards by the introduction of John Minton's landscapes, heralding a taste for looser calligraphic titling and lithographic illustration.

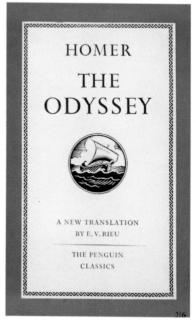

[C17] Advertisements were included in wartime Penguins. During the war a note encouraging readers to pass books on for use by the Armed Services was included.

[C18] The Penguin Classics, introduced in 1946, were designed in the classical tradition, with borders, centralized titles and a wood-engraving.

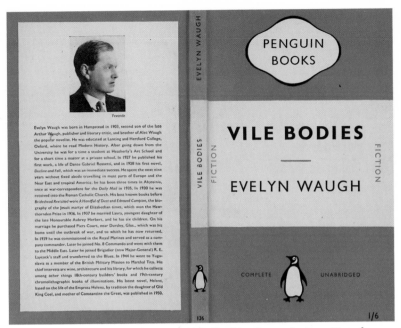

[c19] The revised fiction cover by Jan Tschichold achieved a regular imposition of title and author's name and consistency between spine, rear cover and front cover. A small but significant detail was the line between title and author.

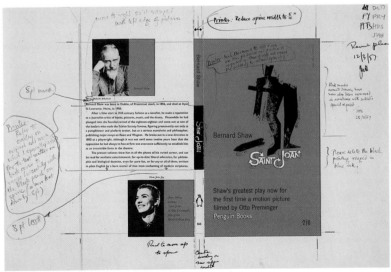

[c20] A written dialogue between printer and typographer in the form of annotations was essential. This example is an unusual film tie-in of 1957, in which Hans Schmoller had incorporated the film-titling from Preminger's *Saint Joan*, designed by Saul Bass.

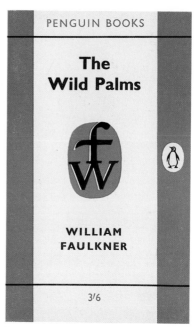

[c21, c22] A vertical format, as shown in the artwork for *Eminent Victorians*, was extended from the Biography series to many Fiction titles. It allowed space for individual treatment, as the example of *The Wild Palms* shows.

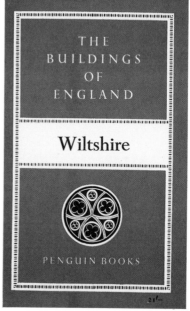

[c23] An illustrated cover for a Handbook by David Gentleman. The style was continued throughout the book with atmospheric vignettes. [c24] By contrast The Buildings of England series was presented in a neo-classical form.

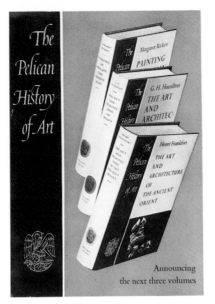

[c25] The first clothbound series, The Pelican History of Art, was designed by Hans Schmoller in 1953 and incorporated a Pelican colophon by Berthold Wolpe. This publicity leaflet made use of the series style.

[c26] Amongst the many pre-war Penguin imitators was the Hutchinson Pocket Library, a reprint series. The covers were also colour-coded, and were primarily typographical.

[c27] For more popular titles a vignette of the action was included, here a drawing by Stephen Russ of 1956.

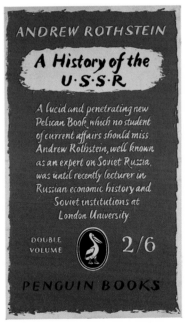

[c28] Until 1960, Penguin point-of-sales material tended to be underplayed, with straightforward information represented in a calligraphic way.

[c29] The first format devised in the United States for Ian Ballantine by Lucian Bernhard in 1942, in this case incorporating a drawing by Busoni.

[c30] Robert Jonas re-designed the series format with the colophon shape indicating genre, in this case square for fiction. Artwork was also often by him.

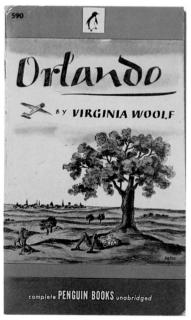

[c31] George Salter's illustration for *Orlando* reflected pictorial interests in the United States. Salter's Germanic training was apparent in the titling, a style he was teaching at the Cooper Union, New York.

[c32] A conceptual treatment for the Pelican titles was popular with Jonas, who provided most of their covers. The Pelican colophon was drawn by Elaine de Kooning in 1946.

[c33, top left] Abram Games, as Consultant Art Director from 1956 to 1958, introduced a format which was reminiscent of early American Penguins. It allowed sufficient space for a pictorial element, whether conceptual or illustrative. [c34, top right, c35] Patterned papers were a popular application for the Music Scores and the Poetry series. Those shown are by Stephen Russ [c34] and Elizabeth Friedländer [c35], the former imitating a fabric pattern.

[c36] A fluency of pictorial reference was acknowledged by matching a painting to a title, an idea which Germano Facetti introduced in 1962.

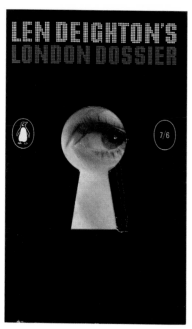

[c37] Obscure or humorous covers became part of the formula, as with this use of a photograph of Twiggy in 1967.

[c38] Filmic and television qualities were reproduced on book covers. Photomontage was used here in a design by Alan Spain in 1964.

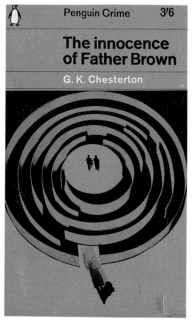

[c39] Romek Marber's grid provided a house-style open to broad graphic possibilities. It was first introduced for the Crime series in 1962.

[c40] The Penguin identity was established in the High Street by Penguin paperback bookshops and shops within shops, this one designed by Germano Facetti. The assertion of colour and a coherent style were two essential qualities between 1961 and 1965.

PENGUIN MODERN POETS 8   Edwin Brock
Geoffrey Hill
Stevie Smith

[c41] A variation on the Marber grid was used for the striking Modern Poets cover, with still-life close-ups of plants and other natural elements, making a contemporary pastoral.

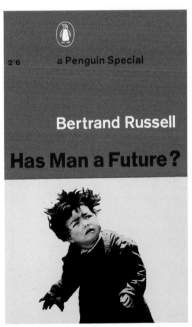

2/6   a Penguin Special

Bertrand Russell

Has Man a Future?

[c42] Penguin Specials were of major importance in the renewed social engagement of the early sixties. Design was streamlined, assertive and reduced to essentials.

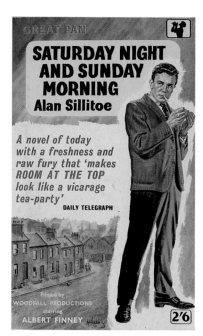

[c43, c44] A contrast of film tie-ins shows Penguin's restrained response. A John Braine edition of 1959 is shown here with an Alan Sillitoe edition of 1960 by Pan Books.

[c45, c46] Two Penguin Modern Classics showing the early format in which either a commissioned line-drawing or a drawing by an earlier artist, in this case George Grosz, was used [c45]. Later colour reproductions of paintings became popular. Here the grey of the Penguin Modern Classics is changed to black, giving full impact to the painting. A similar solution, with sans-serif titling, was applied to the Classics [c73].

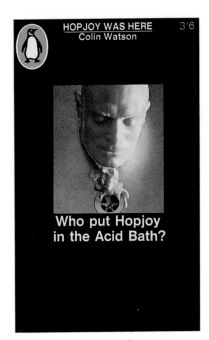

[c47–c50] Alan Aldridge introduced text on the covers which would intrigue the customer. Between 1963 and 1967, as Fiction Art Director, he also commissioned photographs of unusual locations and contributed his own characteristic fluid airbrush drawings.

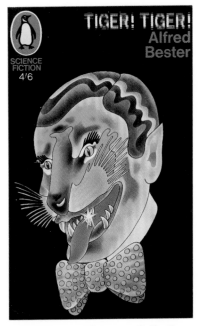

[c49, c50] Coinciding with Pop Art in Britain, this tendency to treat each cover individually acknowledged different marketing forces for different categories of fiction.

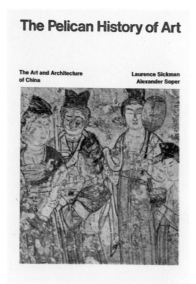

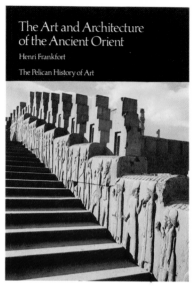

[c51, c52] Two Pelican History of Art volumes, as first designed in paperback in 1966 (left), and as later revised (right) in the early 1970s, showing the changing attitudes towards choice of typography (from Helvetica to Palatino), layout and organization of the photograph.

[c53, c54] *Twelfth Night* in the American Pelican Shakespeare series, showing Fritz Kredel's design. On the right, a leaflet introducing the *Complete Pelican Shakespeare* of 1969, designed by Hans Schmoller.

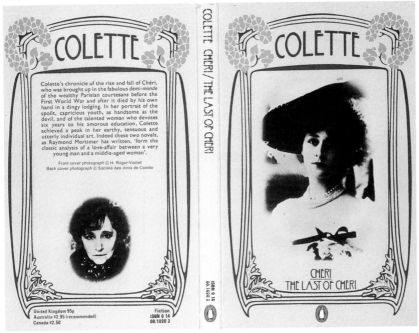

[c55] A period treatment for the Colette series using a design derived from Hector Guimard. By 1970 the entire cover was open to the interpretation of the commissioned designer.

[c56, c57] Cartoons and ideas from animation were integrated into book design, as with Mel Calman's sensitive treatment (left), and Peter Fluck and Roger Law's models (right). Both benefited from the open grid, which guaranteed the series identity by title and colophon as well as by spine.

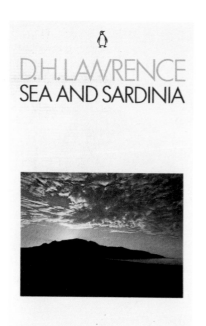

[c58, c59] Attention to typographical titling was characteristic, whether in the conflation of the 'A' and 'W' in the Lawrence series, or the more straightforward treatment of the New English Dramatists by Henning Boehlke.

[c60, c61] Period treatment, using either a new design, here by Peter Bentley for the Waugh books, or filmic or photographic elements, as in the Chandler, coincided with popular nostalgia and revivalism in the early seventies.

[c62] Derek Birdsall and Harri Peccinotti's design for the W. Somerset Maugham series of 1971, in which a still-life was carried over from one title to another, reflected ideas applied in packaging at this time.

[c63] Penguin Education and Education Specials were characterized by black and white covers. Occasionally a pun on the title was made. Otherwise, as here, a salient emblem was found.

[c64] David King's designs for the Marx Library used bold primary colours and cropped grainy photography, reflecting an interest in Soviet Constructivist designs of the 1920s.

[c65–c68] A recasting of identity was made in the C. S. Forester series, to convey their sense of adventure, in 1980. *The Far Pavilions* required a cover treatment uncharacteristic of Penguin when it was introduced in 1979. For the Graham Greene series, the scale of typography and its relation to the illustration was altered, in order to attract attention.

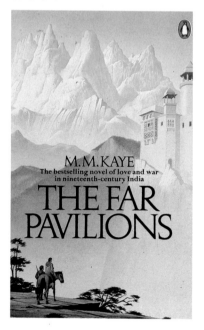

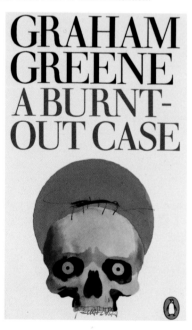

[c69–c72] A revival in illustration occurred in the late 1970s, as indicated by the covers for the King Penguin series, introduced in 1982, and the revised Modern Classics and Peregrines. c69 by Liz Pyle, c70 by Andrzej Klimowski, c71 by Tom Woodruff and c72 by Ed Lindlof.

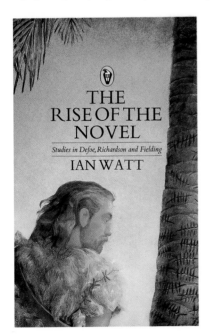

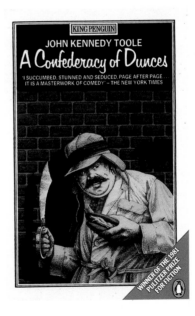

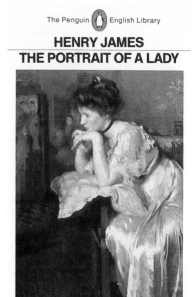

[c73, c74] The black Classics covers, introduced in 1963 by Germano Facetti with Standard or Helvetica typeface, gave a clear, functional design. There was an adaptation of this formula for the English Library as well as for the grey Modern Classics [see c45].

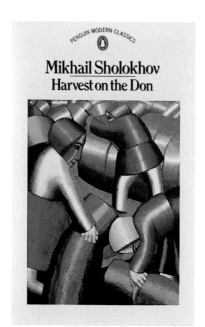

[c75, c76] Continuity and change: The larger-format Modern Classics now have a central title and an inset reproduction. Commissioned portraits, many, as here, by Lawrence Mynott, are the feature of the new series Lives and Letters.

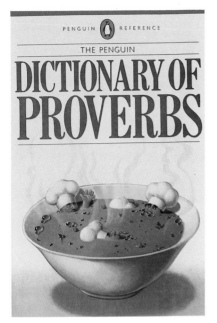
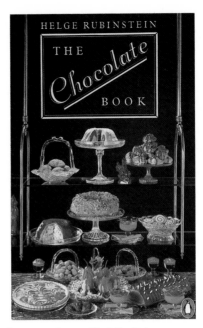

[c77, c78] Continuity and change: The Reference Library as redesigned by Mike Dempsey and Ken Carroll allowed room for an illustration, here by Bob Haberfield [c77]; the cookery Handbooks have become associated with imaginative photographic still-lifes.

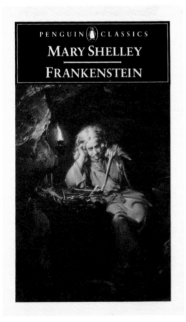

[c79, c80] The most recent revision of the Classics covers, designed by Steve Kent, the present Art Director, for production in 1985, signified a return to centred design. However the policy to include a reproduction of a painting is continued, as it also is in the Poetry Library.

[c81–c84] The tradition of illustration and design for Puffin Story Books has been to provide different interpretations of realism and fantasy. At the same time they have been given as much typographical attention as the various adult series have, as the cover of *A Puffin Quartet of Poets*, originally published in 1958, shows.

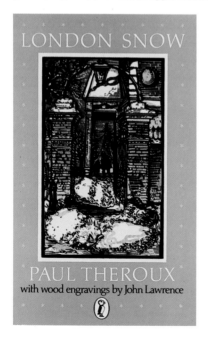

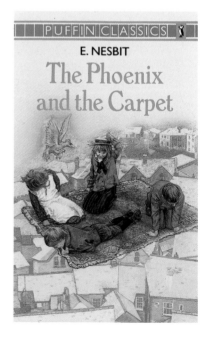

which Lotte Reiniger designed for *The Tales of King Arthur*, seemed appropriate. In another case, the reportage approach of sketchy, spontaneous figures was applied to Eleanor Graham's adaptation of *The Story of Jesus*, bringing life to a potentially difficult subject. The illustrator, Brian Wildsmith, commented that there are

roughly two ways of illustrating a book. The first is to give, shall we say, a diagrammatic representation of the text, the sole aim being to put the text into picture form; the other is to enlarge on the text, to create a pictorial form that is at one with the text and yet is a thing unto itself. (M. Hoffmann and E. Samuels, *Authors and Illustrators of Children's Books*, Bowker, New York, 1972, p. 415)

Mostly the latter solution was appropriate in Puffin books, especially for younger readers.

This Puffin policy of restrained but serious children's publishing continued, once the formula had been established, until the early sixties.

EARLY ART AND DESIGN PUBLISHING AT PENGUIN

In the early Pelican list, one trend, which was supported by Allen Lane and reinforced by the editors, was towards the visual arts. This became more evident during the war, when several new series specifically addressed the field of art and design. The first of these, Penguin Modern Painters (April 1944), was intended as a reasonably priced library of modern painters, with an emphasis on the younger British generation. Part of the books' popularity may have been in showing paintings at a time when the national collections had been evacuated. The editor was the then Director of the National Gallery, Kenneth Clark. He commissioned editions on Graham Sutherland and Henry Moore, later followed by Paul Nash, both William and Ben Nicholson, Edward Bawden and Frances Hodgkins [c13]. The first European, Paul Klee, did not appear until 1949, and despite plans for an American series to be edited by Alfred Barr and James Thrall Soby of the Museum of Modern Art, New York, only Ben Shahn's and Edward Hopper's work was actually published. *Georges Braque* (1959) seemed to indicate a change, but was in fact the last of the series.

Modern Painters were in landscape format with an introductory essay set in double columns and a clear plates list; they contained sixteen colour and sixteen black-and-white illustrations, and the early design and production were overseen by Ruari McLean. After 1949, they were one of various series to be produced in a more durable hard cover, with a typographic design covered in turn by a coloured photographic dust-jacket.

The Times Literary Supplement noticed their propagandist slant:

One great advantage of this series is that at a moderate cost it will enable people who have not the time or the opportunity to keep up with contemporary art exhibitions to see for themselves what other people are making all the fuss about. (Quoted on the cover of Penguin Modern Painters 13, *Ben Nicholson*)

The series may be seen to have taken up many of the debates on modern art which had been rehearsed during the thirties in the pages of the *Listener* and the *Left Review* and among the various newly formed groups of artists and designers. The editorial policy of the Modern Painters demonstrated that part of Penguin's interpretation of general knowledge was a familiarity with European ideas of abstraction and surrealism in painting and their relevance to all areas of three-dimensional design, a subject which had been previously considered the preserve of a cultural élite.

Another venture at the time was the series of Penguin Prints, colour reproductions of paintings accompanied by a short essay on the work. Their selection was again in the charge of Kenneth Clark and included works by Cézanne, Klee, Picasso, Palmer and Turner. The choice implied an uncertainty about the nature of the potential customer. With this, and the difficulty of marketing prints in bookshops, as well as the lack, at the time, of alternative places to sell them, the series can be considered only a limited success.

With the concerns of Penguin editors W. E. Williams and H. L. Beales in workers' education and the part Penguin played in publishing books which anticipated the issues of the Beveridge Report of 1942, a case can be made that some of Penguin's war publications played an important part in the debate leading to the formation of the Welfare State and its related bodies, the Arts Council and Design

THE THINGS WE SEE—No. 5

PUBLIC
TRANSPORT

PENGUIN BOOKS

5. *A typical page from* Furniture *by Gordon Russell, in* The Things We See *series, showing the use of photographic evidence as argument.*

6. *The cover of* The Things We See No. 5, *showing the incorporation of the 'eye', designed by Richard Guyatt in* 1949.

Council. Two series, Planning, Design and Art (from 1942) and The Things We See (from 1947), illustrate this further. The former had among its titles *Living in Cities* by the architect Ralph Tubbs (who had also designed Penguin's offices and warehouse at Harmondsworth), *The County of London Plan* by Ernö Goldfinger and E. J. Carter, *Homes by the Million* by Hugh Casson and Bertil Hultén's *Building Modern Sweden* [c14]. Such titles coincided with post-war reconstruction and town-planning prior to the most popular manifestation of this movement at the Festival of Britain in 1951. As they concerned architecture and planning, it was necessary to incorporate diagrammatic and photographic illustrations. Varieties of layout were tried, possibly under the impetus of *Picture Post*; for example, photographs were used to argue a case on their own (Figure 5).

A spirit of evangelism and self-improvement pervaded the series The Things We See, a short sequence of books, important in the story of Penguin's design for their imaginative covers and page designs:

They run to 64 pages, and are profusely and beautifully illustrated. They are marvels of the

printer's and publisher's art, and should prove extremely popular . . . They are aids to informed understanding, can be used as text books and to provide subjects for discussion in study circles, they direct the eye and mind to a cultural discrimination, and all this with subtle wit, based on expert knowledge. (British Journal of Photography, as quoted on the dust-jacket)

That continental Modernism was a source of this 'discrimination' is supported by the emphasis on functionalism and on the social responsibility of the designer, as well as by the telling 'eye' on the cover of the early editions which had originated in many German and Soviet designs of the 1920s (Figure 6).

A contrasting series but complementary to the Modern Painters was John Lehmann's *New Writing*, originally begun in 1936 as an anthology of essays, stories and poetry by writers of the Left. Lehmann turned to Allen Lane for support in 1940, and on acceptance the series became *Penguin New Writing*. At its height, the magazine reached printings of more than 75,000 copies, appearing regularly until its fortieth volume in September 1950. Its demise was hastened by the revival of magazine publishing after the war, but it had also inevitably reached the natural lifespan of such a series.

The teaming of Allen Lane and John Lehmann was in many respects incongruous. Lehmann belonged to a world which, for all his experience at The Bodley Head and for all the confidence given by increasing Penguin success, Allen could never regard as his own; the world of old established artistic families, of the Bloomsbury set, of left-wing elegance . . .

Lehmann offered no concession to populism, and Allen Lane demanded none. Only price, format and frequency of publication differentiated it from its parent publication . . . Allen Lane had his own Yellow Book at last. (J. P. Morpurgo: *Allen Lane, King Penguin*, Hutchinson, 1979)

Penguin New Writing began with a confident adaptation of the Penguin cover format; a strong black grid with thick colour contrasts, reminiscent of De Stijl minimal designs. However, at its twenty-seventh issue the cover changed to a softened calligraphic interpretation, with the insertion of a landscape. This landscape and the illustrations commissioned for inside the book were in the tradition of the Seven and Five Society, with only a slight Surrealist or Cubist inflection. The *Yellow Book* could be invoked in comparison for its similarity as a literary magazine; however, the tone, subjects and imagery differed considerably [c15 and c16].[3]

CLASSICAL TYPOGRAPHY AND BOOK DESIGN

Although the series mentioned above could be considered examples of prestige publishing, showing that Penguin was diversifying the layout of its books and developing skills in colour reproduction, the usual Penguin volume, whether a novel, poetry, a play or a reference book, depended on clear typographical design. Penguin, like other paperback houses, had followed the principle that typography was good if it could be easily read and, at best, read without the recognition that it had been 'designed'.

With this in mind Allen Lane had noticed inconsistencies in Penguin's production,

3. An account of the artistic debates of the period and especially the reception of Modernism are given in Charles Harrison: *English Art and Modernism 1900–1939*, Allen Lane/Indiana, 1981.

partly as a result of the restrictions imposed by war shortages and partly because of the evolutionary stages by which the series had developed. Early on in the war Penguin had secured a sufficient paper allowance to remain profitably in business by taking September 1938 to August 1939, a year in which a number of new Penguin series had been launched and Penguin Specials were selling in hundreds of thousands, as the annual basis of rationing for its production. The war had taken its toll on binding, which changed from sewn to stapled, and on the arrangement of the text, which was cramped and heavy at times. Advertisements had been incorporated on the backs of the covers and also inside the books [c17]. The colophon had developed into an overweight, dancing bird. Keen to reassert a coherence for the series, Allen Lane consulted Oliver Simon of The Curwen Press about who might be the best typographer to reform the entire series, the most recent being the Penguin Classics, launched in January 1946 by E. V. Rieu's translation of *The Odyssey* [c18]. Simon recommended the German designer Jan Tschichold, resident in Switzerland, who had most recently revised the Birkhäuser Classics. This series included a ten-volume Shakespeare and a twelve-volume Goethe; it was a pocket series using linen spines and patterned-paper sides and, occasionally, leather binding.

Tschichold had begun his career as a book designer in Germany in 1924 advocating the functionalist principles of the New Typography, which entailed the use of asymmetry, sans-serif typefaces, photographic illustration and, when used, primary colours instead of tinted papers. In the next decade he had published the most important arguments for, and examples of, this approach to industrial book production. In 1934 Tschichold had revised his ideas in favour of what he was to call later, in an article submitted to the International Constructive Art Review *Circle* of 1937, the New Traditionalism. It was this which he would apply to design Penguin's house-style. In contrast to the evident designed quality of the New Typography, Tschichold arrived at Penguin believing that the page layout and organization of a book, if properly carried out, should be unnoticed. Instead of the asymmetry of his earlier work, he recommended centred titling, typographical variety with changes in weight and range of typefaces, and decorated borders on covers. British designers would have known Jan Tschichold's work from his previous visit in 1937, when he had worked for Lund Humphries in collaboration with R. B. Fishenden on *The Penrose Annual* for 1938.

Before arriving at Penguin, Tschichold requested examples of all the Penguin series. The set of *Composition Rules* (Figure 7) was the summation of his revisions and allowed his impact to be seen in every book. It consisted of design specifications for the typography department and printers to follow. Allen Lane had insisted that the general scheme of the fiction titles, their colour, tripartite design and Gill Sans-Serif, should be kept in order to preserve the brand identity. However, within this constraint Tschichold reproportioned the colour-bands and improved the imposition of title, author and colophon, ensuring that it would be consistent between volumes. The colophon was redrawn in eight variations. Tschichold recommended that the optical spacing of the titling should be improved and made consistent [C19].

When it came to the text, there were further rules:

– *Words should be set as closely as possible always, and if this means breaking a word, this is preferable to spacing being too wide, which would allow holes in the page and slow the reader down.*
– *No extra space should be given after full stops.*
– *Paragraphs should be indented ... by one em of the body of the type being used.*
– *Words in capitals should be letter-spaced but large capitals optically spaced.*

(Abridged from *Penguin Composition Rules*, 1947)

The mention of 'rules' should not convey the impression that the typography was applied in a rigid or inflexible way. Within these ground-rules each book was designed separately, its typeface, tone of page and finer detail such as headings, borders and chapter openings varying according to the subject. Such a blend of standardization and variety became an essential ingredient of Penguin typography, recognized by the awards given by the National Book League. However, it was a costly exercise, which could be justified in 1949 only by print runs of 20,000 or over:

Penguin Composition Rules

First issued 1947, revised 1951, 1956, 1958, 1961, 1964, 1970, 1972
Further revised 1983
All previous editions cancelled

These rules, with the help of our printers, have played an appreciable part in raising the standard of composition and ensuring consistency in our publications. Further copies can be obtained from the Production Department, Penguin Books Ltd, 536 King's Road, London SW10 0UH (telephone: 01-351 2393). If there are any queries arising from these instructions, or from a particular manuscript, contact the Chief Designer or the Managing Editor at the address above.

Since film-setting terminology varies from printer to printer, spacing instructions given are for hot-metal setting.

TEXT COMPOSITION

All text composition should be closely word-spaced. As a rule, the spacing should be about a middle space or the thickness of an 'i' in the type size used.

Wide spaces should be strictly avoided. Words may be broken whenever necessary to avoid wide spacing, as this is less harmful to the appearance of the page than too much space between words. An effort should, however, be made to avoid more than two successive hyphens and hyphens at the end of pages, particularly recto pages.

All major punctuation marks – full point, colon and semicolon – should be followed by the same spacing as is used in the rest of the line.

INDENTING OF PARAGRAPHS

Paragraphs should be indented one em of the body of the type used.

Omit indents in the first line of the first paragraph of any text and at the beginning of a new section that comes under a sub-heading. It is not necessary to set the first word in small capitals, but if this has been specified, the word should be letter-spaced in the same way as the running headlines, if any.

If a chapter is divided into several parts without headings, these parts

1

---

7. *The* Penguin Composition Rules *have been updated and revised from time to time since 1947 to take account of technological developments.*

Typographically the pocket edition in paper covers presents many problems and standardization of size does not mean the designer cannot refine his plan to the utmost. The following example will show this: a printer's bill of £160 for corrections, partly of a typographical nature (fine adjustment in leading, spacing, and many revisions before arriving at the final form of the title and preliminary pages), would spell the economic ruin of a book with an edition of say 3,000 copies. But in an edition of 50,000 or 100,000 the total cost of production is such that £160 will not seriously prejudice the profit and loss account. (Hans Schmoller: *Printing Review*, Spring 1951)

Such adjustments, deemed to be necessary aesthetically on the arrival of proofs from the printers, had to justify themselves economically. The conclusion is that Allen Lane wanted good typography and was prepared to pay for it. However, a broader conclusion may be drawn that design for mass-production frequently requires such an initial substantial investment.

Tschichold's impact was stimulating, painful, almost alarming. No detail of production was overlooked, but it was in the composing room that his influence was most strongly felt – meticulous and immensely detailed layouts were followed by revises without number and even personal visits. (Elliott Viney in *Penguins Progress 1935–1960*, Penguin Books, 1960, p. 24)

Elliott Viney was one of the major printers of Penguin Books. His view was amplified by Tschichold's own comments on his difficulty in adapting to British printing:

They obviously understood nothing of what I meant by the spacing of capitals. As I often had a veritable mountain of corrections to look through (sometimes ten a day), I had the following rubber stamp made: 'Equalize letter spaces according to their optical value'. This stamp was practically never noticed. (Quoted in Ruari McLean: *Jan Tschichold: Typographer*, Lund Humphries, 1975, pp. 144–7)

The arguments rehearsed here were gradually resolved by practice and compromise. Other tasks and decisions were to arise for the typographic designer with changes in publishing patterns within Penguin, when smaller editions of more specialized titles became necessary, and with the advent of film-setting. Filmset books which originated as hardbacks could be adapted to paperback production using the same text layouts. The design of the page had then to take account of the different requirements of a paperback page.

In 1949 Tschichold returned to Switzerland and was succeeded by the book designer Hans Schmoller, who had most recently been working for The Curwen Press. This press, run by Oliver Simon and Harold Curwen, had been a major patron of both modernist and traditional illustration in the interwar years. As well as this, its name was associated with the reform of book design; since the formation of the Design and Industries Association in 1915, Curwen had been keen to apply its principles of 'fitness for purpose' to publishing. With the experience of his German training and work at The Curwen Press, Hans Schmoller was a most suitable designer to maintain Penguin's reputation for refined typography.

Shortly after his arrival Schmoller recalls seeing a sketch for a proposed revision for the covers by the assistant typographer Erik Frederiksen, based on a vertical panel and coloured border. The panel in the centre allowed room for a small amount of copy, a drawing or photograph and a variation in the typeface. Until now most Penguin covers had been set in Gill Sans-Serif. Schmoller was to experiment with all of these possibilities.

Now suitable for front-forward display, the Fiction list could be broken down to author identities, which particularly fitted the 'Tens' – sets of ten titles, each set amounting to one million books, by the same author published simultaneously. The first author to be treated in this way was Bernard Shaw, in 1946. Initially the vertical panel was introduced to encourage the sales of biographies, as in the case of Lytton Strachey's *Eminent Victorians* [c21]. Imre Reiner's elegant Corvinus, a serif typeface designed in 1931, was used for Aldous Huxley. Other author series were distinguished by graphic emblems: for example, Berthold Wolpe was commissioned to design a monogram for the William Faulkner titles [c22]. The Crime series, however, maintained its original conception.

The vertical format was perhaps incorporated most successfully in the Penguin Handbooks, in which a coloured border was decorated by line-drawings, sometimes printed in non-registering colours. Illustrators from the Royal College of Art would provide free-style evocative line-drawings of the sort which had become popular following the Festival of Britain in 1951. In all fields of design, from interior decoration to ceramics, a taste for surface-pattern was replacing the rigour of the Modern Movement and the austerity of the war years alike. The Handbooks reflected this softening, both in their covers and in their subjects. A domestic 'lifestyle' was offered which acknowledged the popularity of foreign holidays and was particularly Francophile, as Elizabeth David's cookery books epitomized [c23]. Increased leisure time and car ownership may have partly helped another series which began in July 1951. Nikolaus Pevsner had suggested a series of architectural guides based on the Dehio Handbücher der Kunstdenkmäler, a German edition of four volumes which he remembered from his days at

Göttingen University. The original intention was for the Penguin series to replace the Penguin Guides, to be called the Buildings of England and to be completed within ten years, but the scale and detail of the project subsequently increased enormously.

Produced in paperback and with protective paper dust-covers, the Buildings of England fitted perfectly in jacket pockets, and Pevsner's combination of meticulous research and strong opinion* suited their readers, who usually built up a collection of the full series. In 1951, the average print-run per county was 25,000. Like other reference books, they depended on a very clear and consistent organization of the page [c24 and Figure 8]. However, this was still within the range of one typographer, whether Schmoller or an assistant, who would mark up the manuscript for the composing room, organize title page, end pages and indices, then check the galleys and page-proofs.

In 1953, again under the editorship of Nikolaus Pevsner, the Pelican History of Art began [c25]. This series was intended to achieve the comprehensiveness of the Buildings of England, this time covering the art and architecture of the world. It was unique in Penguin's publishing at the time because it was conceived as a cloth-bound series. It provided the opportunity to apply typographical care and attention to scholarly reference books, each with an average of 192 half-tone plates and specially drawn illustrations of architectural plans and sections.

A review made at its coming of age in 1956 in *The Penguin Story* could suggest that Penguin at first had depended on its individuality, then its hard-earned consistency, then its development into a cultural institution.

In a sense the free-lance phase of Penguins is over; the adventurous sallies have given way to the solid responsibility of building up a comprehensive Popular Educator. (W. E. Williams, *The Penguin Story*, Penguin Books, 1956, p.60)

This progress can be charted by the various reactions to the problem of Penguin's identity. For example, Allen Lane was reluctant that 'Penguin' should be adopted as the generic term for any paperback at the risk that other less carefully produced paperbacks might

8. *A typical page layout for Pevsner's Buildings of England, in this case by Hans Schmoller for Wiltshire (1963).*

detract from this identity. The chain of Penguin imitators had, on the other hand, reinforced rather than weakened the popularity of the formula [c26]. Characteristic of the security which Penguin's identity encouraged was W. E. Williams' comment on the possibility of adapting to American style packaging and advertising, also made in the twenty-first anniversary publication:

The most familiar feature of the Penguin look is, of course, the avoidance of pictorial covers. In America the lurid cover is considered essential for securing mass sales of paper-backed books; and in this country also, most of the cheap reprints are presented in picture covers. It has often been urged that Penguins might do better business if it conformed to this general practice; but whatever truth there may be in that supposition, the decision has been made, as a matter of taste, to reject the

American kind of cover. (The Penguin Story, Penguin Books, 1956, p.26)

A small amount of copy, or an illustration highlighting the adventurous aspect of the more popular titles such as John Buchan's novels, had been allowed on the covers, although the lists and the booksellers' cards were still calligraphic or typographical [c27 and c28]. Likewise, advertisements in *The Times Literary Supplement* of new and forthcoming titles were uncompromisingly straightforward, embellished by variety in the typeface rather than by advertiser's copy. However, a request from booksellers for more varied covers reflected the gradual recognition that books, like any other consumer product, would need to be packaged and positively marketed, an awareness affected by a developing knowledge of American sales techniques.

In order to fulfil this request, and to guarantee that in the face of mounting competition authors did not move to other publishers, cover policy had to be changed. Accompanying this development was the recognition that the publishing company offering the highest advance would acquire the author's work.

THE CHALLENGE OF CONSUMERISM: PENGUIN INC.

Despite publishing large editions of popular books, Penguin had remained a minority publisher, as opposed to a mass-market paperback company, during its first twenty-one years in Britain. However, Allen Lane had been interested in the possibility of marketing in the United States from the beginning and, if this was to succeed, an assessment of the British Penguin approach to marketing would be required.

In July 1939 Penguin's New York office was established by Allen Lane, to import and distribute British-originated books. In charge was Ian Ballantine, a young American publisher. At first the operation was primarily a matter of gauging which titles from the Penguins, Pelicans and Specials lists would sell. However, after Pearl Harbor, the submarine blockades and the subsequent entry of the United States into the war, importing became increasingly difficult. Kurt Enoch,

with his experience of an English-language reprint series at Albatross Books, was appointed as Vice-President in charge of production by Allen Lane during a visit to New York in 1941, a move which would help when it was decided to publish Penguins in the United States.

Obviously wartime book production rested on dependable paper supplies, and Penguin Inc. astutely secured a number of agreements with the United States Government which assured it access to supplies in the United States while most British publishers suffered. For instance, co-production with the *Infantry Journal*, a publication of the Military Service Publishing Company, meant that a considerable part of Penguin's production was of books about the war. This subsidized a more important aspect of future Penguin policy in the United States, the increasing publication of American literature, whether classics such as Walt Whitman's *Leaves of Grass* or works by more recent writers, William Faulkner and Carson McCullers among them. This policy reflected the editorial influence of Victor Weybright, who had joined Enoch as Editorial Director in 1945. The revised format in which Penguins began to appear in 1942 was designed by Lucian Bernhard, the renowned German *émigré* graphic designer [c29]. The first crop of books signified a break with British Penguins in size and layout but, more importantly, in the use of pictorial covers. This move towards the active marketing of books was undoubtedly governed by the form of paperback distribution which operated in the United States, where paperbacks were 'piggybacked' on national magazine distribution organized by regional wholesalers. On average 70 per cent of books were sold and 30 per cent returned to be pulped.

From their inception in 1939, more paperbacks were sold through railway stations, drugstores and news-stands in the United States than through conventional bookshops, and Penguins competed on the shelf with Pocket Books, the first American paperback imprint, and other series, each with a pictorial formula. Colour-coding was continued in the Penguin Inc. Bernhard design, but the colours were different: maroon for Fiction, dark green for Mystery, yellow for Biography, orange for Penguin Specials, and blue for all the others,

including Poetry. A border running from front
to back, space for the author's biography and
photograph and an inset illustration became
standard design characteristics. A European
feature was the preference shown for calligraphic titling, which would complement the
illustration and vary between titles, very
different from the typographical solution in
Britain.

The commercial artist Robert Jonas was
probably responsible for the revision of the
various series introduced in 1946. This
entailed a switch to the standard format,
known as 'A' format from 1975 in Britain,
which is roughly the same as 'M' format in the
United States. Jonas worked as 'type-director'
for Victor Weybright and Kurt Enoch. He
also designed a considerable amount of the
cover artwork, while Gobin Stair handled art
direction until 1946. Jonas found the im-
migration of European designers an important factor in the development of his style,
which was to favour collage and photographic
montage as well as hand-drawn illustration.
For three years, between 1946 and 1948,
American Penguins and Pelicans lost their
colour-coding: instead, genre was indicated by
the shape in which the colophon appeared: a
square for Fiction, a triangle for Crime and
Detection, a circle for Poetry and Anthologies
and a diamond for Miscellaneous [c30 and
c31].

Familiar with the social realism of New
Deal paintings but also with the continental
Modernism of Herbert Bayer, Moholy-Nagy
and E. McKnight Kauffer, Jonas produced
conceptual covers using montage to evoke the
atmospheric equivalent of a novel, and found
salient thematic emblems for the Pelicans, as
in *Patterns of Culture* by Ruth Benedict [c32].
None the less a change in taste towards
figuration and away from more experimental
covers had occurred by 1950, when Jonas's
early covers were repackaged, their original
covers hidden in dust-covers on which easel
paintings of the 'commercial' variety were
reproduced. Fear of such a development and
a distaste for the packaging and promotion
of books as it existed in America caused a
rift between Allen Lane and Penguin U.S.A.
According to an agreement made in late 1947,
the name Penguin would be combined with
Signet, Pelican with Mentor, and after one

year the American directors of Penguin, Kurt
Enoch and Victor Weybright, would publish
under the umbrella of the New American
Library of World Literature. Penguin Books
Inc. did not appear again until 1950 and
then mainly as an import and distribution
subsidiary based in Baltimore rather than
New York, and safely managed by a British
president, Harry Paroissien. The New
American Library, in the meantime, began its
operation as one of the largest and most highly
respected of the many American paperback
houses.

PENGUIN IN BRITAIN 1957–60

Even with vignettes British Penguin did not
secure face-forward display in bookshops. The
introduction of pictorial covers fell outside the
role of a book designer, as Hans Schmoller
practised it, so in 1956 he appointed Abram
Games as Consultant Art Director to oversee
this development with selected titles. Games
had been associated with modern graphic
design since his work on Ministry of Information posters; after 1945 he had worked
freelance, teaching at the Royal College of
Art in the newly formed Graphic Design
Department, and he had been further recognized for designs for the Festival of Britain and
the BBC.

The titles chosen for pictorial treatment
(thirty-six altogether) ranged from popular
comic novels, such as *Clochemerle* and *Whisky
Galore*, to westerns and adventure stories. In
all probability they were intended as bestsellers, although they were promoted simply
by a small display card to stand on bookshop
counters. Games provided a format in which
an illustration could be inserted as the main
element of the front cover [c33]. A variation of
the family Gill Sans-Serif typeface was used for
title, author and imprint title: 'Penguin Books'
appeared on the front reversed-out on the
illustration and also on the back cover.
Penguin's identity was further reinforced by
use of Tschichold's colophon. A place for a
biographical paragraph and a photograph of
the author was provided in the asymmetric
layout on the back cover.

The artwork for some of the covers was
produced by Games, but for others either
recently graduated designers or illustrators,

such as Pat Keely, Dennis Bailey and Edwin Tatum, were commissioned from the Royal College of Art or more established designers like Hans Unger were employed. The results, using an abstract vocabulary, showed a similarity to more advanced poster design. In this respect, many parallels can be drawn between this series and Robert Jonas's series ten years earlier in New York: both found designers who were familiar with the Modern Movement in graphic design.

Some of the covers were considered too sophisticated to sell:

Looking back over the first years of the Penguin pictorial covers, they seem, in the majority, to be miscast. Ranging from the stunning and brilliant down to the merely first-rate, these popular mass-market titles have been dressed far above their station in life. Indeed many of the pictorial covers are above the heads of the bookshop public. (Tony Godwin: 'Survival of the Slickest', *Book Design and Production*, 1958, p. 35)

More importantly it became evident from sales figures that the series did not justify the costs of four-colour reproduction, and it was abruptly stopped in 1958, following an editorial meeting, without prior warning to the designers.

STANDARDIZATION OR INDIVIDUALITY? 1960–67

Standardization in Design

Although further moves towards finding a younger readership were made, especially by John Curtis, from 1953 to 1961, with experimental formats and covers, it was not until the new grid commissioned in 1961 for the Crime series that a modern and consistent look was achieved, which would spread to all the series. In the books commissioned by Curtis, when he doubled as Fiction Art Editor, a new stable of designers had been located, ready to apply experimental ideas. These ideas reflected a growing recognition that graphic design could incorporate type and image brought together on a conceptual rather than an illustrative level. The redesigned magazines (*Man About*) *Town*, *Queen* and *Topic* of 1958, and later the launch of the *Sunday Times Supplement* in 1962, presented to the public an increased fluency of images which television

and film had begun to encourage. Instead of the Fabian carefulness which had characterized Penguin from 1935, readers would now be as familiar with kitchen-sink grainy East-End London and Northern England as with Left-Bank cosmopolitan writers. It was the age of free-form jazz, CND and satire [c36 and c37].

In London focal points for this post-war generation had been the bookshops Better Books in Charing Cross Road and, later, Bumpus in Baker Street. Their manager, Tony Godwin, had wanted to avoid stuffiness and create an atmosphere in which books could be discovered and enjoyed. There was a combination of blond Scandinavian wood and blown-up photographic portraits of authors for the interior; bright wrapping paper and bookmarks, and the shop's fascia, were designed by John Sewell, then head graphic designer at the BBC. The emphasis of the shop was towards poetry, literature and the visual arts. Godwin also stocked such journals as the *Architectural Review*, *Domus*, *Graphis*, the *New Yorker* and *Novum Gebrauchsgraphik*, which guaranteed a regular kind of customer. In its subsequent years Better Books developed as an alternative bookshop; however, when Tony Godwin joined Penguin as Fiction Editor in May 1960 he turned his acumen for discovering, guiding and shaping a market towards mass-publishing.

The background of Germano Facetti, appointed Penguin Art Director in early 1960, was indicative of the changing design environment in Britain. He had been trained in architecture and art history in Milan. He then worked for *Domus* and the *Architectural Review* and later became responsible for the interior design of Olivetti's British showrooms. The broad visual references that a designer should make are reflected in the acknowledged list of influences on Facetti's work, from Bill Brandt, Herbert Bayer and Adriano Olivetti to Gordon Cullen of the *Architectural Review*.

At its simplest, Facetti's task was to transform Penguin's identity into something more contemporary, appealing to a growing youthful readership, while showing continuity with the firm's past. Each series had to assert its individuality in the marketplace while allowing room for a designer or illustrator to provide a cover which accommodated each title. The Crime series was chosen as the first and most suitable test-case for revision: just as Agatha Christie and Erle Stanley Gardner had proved popular in the previous decade, a new form of spy literature was ascendant by the early 1960s which would make up the list of 'green' titles. The three designers invited to submit suggestions were John Sewell, Derek Birdsall and Romek Marber. Sewell and Birdsall had already designed covers on a freelance basis, but Marber was unknown. Facetti had only recently seen covers by him for *The Economist* which shared an inventive approach towards both graphic imagery and type. Marber supported his entry with a written analysis of the Edward Young format and of his own, as well as a grid which kept to the proportions of the Golden Section, on which the paperback book size was based. He contended that a new book in the existing format went unnoticed unless the title was read in full, and that the format had lost its initial impact. He wanted to maintain 'goodwill to Penguin Books' by emphasizing common design elements: a strong horizontal emphasis, division of white and green elements and consistency in typography. The typeface was changed to Intertype and Standard Medium, but it remained sans-serif and its weight and feel were similar to Gill, while working more effectively in lower-case. The green and white contrast was to be phased out and replaced by overall green once readers were familiar with the changed format. [Compare c38 and c39.]

Marber's solution was adopted and he was contracted to produce twenty covers a year. His taste was for montages, suitably incongruous or mysterious according to the title. Other designers contributing to this and the other series included Derek Birdsall, Alan Fletcher, F. H. K. Henrion, Richard Hollis, Bruce Robertson and Edwin Taylor.

The impact of the grid and its adaptation to other series can be clearly seen in photographs of bookshop interiors [c40]. Altogether thirty-two grids were devised for the different series. The green was retained to encourage a loyalty to the series, but it was lighter and more modern, and heralded the fashion for turquoise, green and orange which reached its climax by 1965 in the nexus of Pop Art posters and magazines. Other Penguin series fell into

line with slight variations [c41]. Penguin Specials, which had slumped to one or two titles a year during the 1950s, resurfaced towards the end of consensus politics. The Berlin Wall, the Chicago riots, Vietnam and domestic social issues were addressed, and to suit the renewed engagement with these debates an abrupt 'tabloid' approach to covers was made [c42]. Lower-case Helvetica, ranged left, red, black, white, sometimes with shocking photographs, either cropped or bled, became the style. This hard-edge approach was facilitated technically by photographic reproduction and dry-transfer lettering which could be applied by the designer at the art-work stage; visually the imagery connected with more aggressive editorial policy, photo-journalism and the TV screen.

The *Lady Chatterley* case in 1960 provided the final challenge to Edwardian establishment values, while giving Penguin its second million-seller, boosting the already impressive Lawrence list and stimulating the launch of Penguin as a public company.

That Britain had woken up was signalled further by a batch of new fiction published by Godwin. The fiction issued by Penguin in 1957, the year of the Angry Young Men, had been relatively safe. P. G. Wodehouse was published in a series of five, shortly followed by Georges Simenon. However, a new strain of writers began to appear in April 1960 with Iris Murdoch; May of the same year saw William Golding, John Wain and Doris Lessing added to the list, followed by Albert Camus (September 1960) and Jean-Paul Sartre (January 1961). The work of the last two authors would form an important part of the Penguin Modern Classics series. The early sixties continued with the publication of David Storey (January 1962), Keith Waterhouse (August 1962), Edna O'Brien (May 1963), and Günter Grass (October 1965).

These changes were fortunate but also necessary. In 1960 forty publishers were producing paperbacks, although only nine were in direct competition with Penguin. The British paperback revolution had begun. Pan, the second largest paperback house, was steadily promoting its bestsellers, such as *Peyton Place* and Ian Fleming's *Goldfinger*, which secured two million sales in 1964. A contrast of approaches can be seen in two covers of similar types of fiction with film tie-ins [c43 and c44]. According to sales statistics in 1964, Penguin's strength was in its considerable backlist; from a stocklist of 2,000 titles it secured 23 million sales, whereas Pan, at smaller operational costs, reached 17 million with 450 titles. In October 1965 E. V. Rieu's *Odyssey* reached the 2 million mark for Penguin. This difference was acknowledged by Pan's publicity manager:

Penguin are complete publishers in paperback. We are middle of the road entertainers. (In an interview with Terry Coleman, *New Society*, 20 May 1965)

In 1961 Godwin introduced the Penguin Modern Classics, securing for paperback reprint modern American, European and British fiction. To denote a change in tone and seriousness, pale grey spines and panels, with commissioned drawings by artists associated with the fine-art end of illustration such as André François, David Gentleman, Paul Hogarth and Duncan Grant, were brought in. While the grey (sometimes grey-green) was usually retained, soon Facetti introduced reproductions of paintings or sculptures which would complement the novel in period and style [c45 and c46]. He remembered such a usage in French textbooks of his childhood in the Édition Bordas Collection Littéraire. At first the matching of a work of art to a novel was carried out by Facetti with the help of a picture library; later Penguin would employ its own picture researcher. The tendency was to be adventurous, using works which might be considered 'difficult', such as modern paintings. The success of the form hinged on the excellent four-colour printing available which guaranteed accurate photographic reproductions. The appropriateness of the paintings reflected Facetti's knowledge of art history. The solution was extended to the Classics, adapted to the striking black format, and also the English Library.

This reassertion of corporate identity was as important as the 1947 revision, but now the context of the books, their promotion and sales, was more complicated. Changes in patterns of selling towards self-service had necessitated a new form of display. Among popular innovations were the Penguin Bookshop and the 'shop within a shop'. The first Penguin Bookshop opened in Heffers in Cambridge in the late 1950s, soon followed by Collet's at 52 Charing Cross Road. The 'shop within a shop' comprised a section devoted to Penguin Books alone, in which the complete series could be stocked, whereas the idea of the Penguin Bookshop was to establish shops entirely of paperbacks. Specially designed wooden shelving, unit-manufactured, was distributed to make a consistent display. Supermarket organization was reflected in the concept:

A Penguin Bookshop makes an irresistible picture to the public because it represents our complete range – or at least the major part of it – in a face-forward display, therefore maximizing impulse purchase. (Penguin Publicity Department Memo, 1963)

Standard book sizes strengthened the overall impact and facilitated shelving. The 1963 list was estimated to occupy 500–600 feet. The provision of these Penguin environments helped the booksellers as well as the publisher: as a Penguin Bookshop, Collet's increased its turnover by 50 per cent, while as a shop within a shop the W. H. Smith branch in Bradford secured a 65 per cent increase in sales in the same year.

Individuality: Pop and its Impact

Over a drink in Soho with the young illustrator Alan Aldridge, Tony Godwin spoke of bringing an established American designer such as Milton Glaser to Penguin to take care of the popular fiction titles. While the combination of Godwin and Facetti had achieved considerable strength in the more traditional territory of Penguins and Pelicans, and opened up new ground with the English Library, the Classics and the Modern Classics, the problem of dealing with the new fiction troubled Godwin. Jokingly Aldridge suggested that he would art direct for a fraction of the sum which had been mentioned, and was accepted.

Alan Aldridge's path to graphic design was typical of what was happening in London in the early sixties. He had attended the Graphic Workshop in Conduit Street, a forum established by the illustrator-designers Bob Gill and Lou Klein, recently arrived from the United States. Through the Workshop Aldridge had met Facetti and Marber, who had set a Penguin book cover as one of the design briefs there. Aldridge had won this and had been subsequently commissioned to do occasional covers freelance. On account of this and his work for the *Sunday Times Supplement*, another important patron of commercial illustrators, Aldridge developed his characteristic drawing style. At twenty-three, Aldridge became head of a separately established Penguin fiction art department in John Street, Holborn. His background as a commercial illustrator distinguished him from previous art directors at Penguin, with their emphasis on design; but it also distinguished him from the Royal College of Art approach to illustration, a style which portrayed a scene from the narrative in an atmospheric manner, which had also been used on Penguin covers. Aldridge, struck by a generation gap, felt the need to 'cheer up Britain'. He intended to 'reach the kids'.

Part of his strategy was to introduce an irreverent quality – humorous, sexual, decorative or fantastic – to the cover design. Aldridge's own style of illustration was to use a fluid, organic line to create exaggerated or composite shapes, slightly reminiscent of Art Nouveau, which was experiencing a revival at the time. For such drawings Harry Willock introduced air-brushed colour, also applied in the decorative lettering which they were to develop together. Working with Dennis Hackett of *Nova* magazine, Aldridge learnt the technique of introducing startling copy which would encourage the reader to pick up a book either through curiosity or shock [c47 and c48].

Other covers were treated photographically. For these Aldridge had to fight to raise the fee for a design to anything between £50 and £100. One editor found himself in a raincoat at night posing as a peeping-tom, peering through an Islington window for Keith Waterhouse's *Jubb* [c49]. Such staged photographs, despite initial resistance, became a popular formula for cover artwork. The move away from conventional illustration was further emphasized by the use of photographic still-lifes and photographs of wax models. A considerable number of these covers were used on existing editions. However, with the growing interest in science fiction, in 1964 a new series was launched. To give the titles a stunning and novel appearance Aldridge

introduced all-black covers, purple and white lettering and his characteristic weird figures [c50]. Tony Godwin would usually brief Aldridge verbally about the books and Aldridge worked from suggestions of the Fiction Art Department, Robyn Wallace and Cherriwyn Magill, as well as from his own ideas. At this stage a picture researcher became an essential part of the team, locating sources and clearing copyright permission.

The covers had gained liveliness and verve. Some members of the public applauded them; others, including some authors, abhorred them to the extent that reversion of rights was occasionally threatened. Attention on the Fiction Art Department was growing and its function as part of a more aggressive identity for Penguin surfaced as a conflict in 1967. It coincided with a reassertion of authority by Allen Lane against younger staff, dubbed 'the whizzkids' by the press. The financial standing of Penguin was not at issue; figures given in an article in *The Times* of 5 May 1967 showed that annual sales had risen from 17 million in 1960 to 26 million in 1966. Instead it was the recurring question of Penguin identity. If this was determined editorially, it was manifested to the bookseller and reader by marketing and design decisions. By 1965 Penguin was competing with 150 British publishers interested in the paperback market, although the eight at the top shared 85 per cent of the market. *The Times* continued:

Penguin remain a unique service to humanity but in the tough world of the 1960s they must come down to earth and make their products attractive in the marketplace.

The question was the interpretation of 'attractive'.

The cover is the selling agent. If Penguin went back to the old cover Smith's would have to refer customers to the pedigree bookseller round the corner.

If the idea of a return to the original typographical cover was inconceivable, so, for Allen Lane, was the idea of packaging books like any other consumer product. Reyner Banham had suggested that:

The cover on a paperback is a come-on packaging job like the box of washing-up powder, except that it tends to have even less relationship to the contents. ('No More Plain Wrappers', *New Society*, 30 June 1966, p.22)

Allen Lane had won enormous respect from retail booksellers for his resistance to highly commercial covers and American distribution methods. In return, Penguin was usually allocated a prime site in the bookshop. Assessing the departure of Tony Godwin in 1967, an event indicative of this crisis, Michael Sissons commented:

Many booksellers throughout the country have no doubt breathed a sigh of relief that due deference has been shown to them, and that, for the time being, Penguins won't be all over the supermarkets. ('Which Way to Revolution?', New Society, 29 June 1967, p.22)

Interestingly in the same review Sissons predicted that Penguin's marketing policy would be guided by how adventurous its competitors were, rather than by an internal decision. This comment would prove prophetic in the early 1970s, with the rise of interest in serious paperback publishing shown by Pan, Granada and other publishers, and the increase in so-called 'radical publishing', formerly the preserve of the Pelican lists and Penguin Specials.

In design terms, with the departure of Tony Godwin and Alan Aldridge, a sobriety was asserted. An interim period before the appointment of the next Fiction Art Director followed, in which the photographic cover was discouraged except for Crime, and illustrated or typographic covers were preferred for Fiction titles. To help re-establish brand identity, assumed to have been diluted over the previous three years, the label 'A PENGUIN BOOK' typeset in Optima 36 point appeared on every fiction cover. Despite its unpopularity with the cover artists and designers, such a policy was intended to unify the list before a more consistent art policy could be formulated. At the same time, the Classics, Pelicans, Poetry and Penguin English Library remained in the Facetti formula.

Offset Lithography and Film-setting

The introduction of offset lithographic machinery for printing Penguin paperbacks had begun in 1961. One advantage of offset over letter-press was that it facilitated the production of books in which photographic illustrations could be integrated with text, rather than printed on special paper as an inset. On a broader front, art books were beginning to appear in larger-format paperback editions. Accordingly Gerald Cinamon redesigned the Pelican History of Art as a paperback series in 1966 and was then responsible for the Style and Civilization series and Pelican architectural titles, all helping Penguin to keep pace with the proliferation of art and architectural books in the mid-sixties.

For the Pelican History of Art, the case-bound volumes were produced alongside large-format white paperbacks, volumes of over six hundred pages with a standard layout of a colour reproduction and white border on the cover, sans-serif series title and smaller author and book title [c51]. A typical page was set in double columns for ease of reading, with black and white reproductions. Such integrated books suited another popular phenomenon, cartoons, first produced at Penguin in 1962. From Ronald Searle to John Lennon, Spike Milligan to the controversial Siné cartoons, Penguin used an integrated and often larger format to satisfy the growing taste for humour and satire. This larger format was originally introduced in 1962 for the Peregrine series, an important list of academic texts with an orientation towards English literature.

Again a more innovatory layout was used by Cinamon in collaboration with John Berger and Jean Mohr to produce books of their photographic essays (Figure 9). Ideas from magazine design and films such as bled photographs, type over image and horizontal shots were incorporated to direct and alter the reader's experience and expectations of the relationship between image and text.

The first list of Allen Lane The Penguin Press appeared in 1967, marking a return (with a few exceptions) to hardback publishing for Allen Lane thirty-three years after The Bodley Head days. The publication of hardback books raised the question of co-production, which was to become increasingly crucial to hardback and paperback houses alike in the following decade, for the first time at Penguin. As Tschichold had produced a set of *Composition Rules* to coordinate paperback design, so in 1972 Hans Schmoller devised guidelines to design for co-production. If compatible design could be achieved, composition costs would be substantially reduced. Problems arising varied

Landscapes can be deceptive.
Sometimes a landscape seems to be less a setting
for the life of its inhabitants than a curtain behind which
their struggles, achievements and accidents take place.

*9. A double-page photograph with text
superimposed for Berger and Mohr's*
A Fortunate Man, *designed by Gerald Cinamon
in* 1969.

from alterations in the margin widths and the choice of typeface for subheadings to larger considerations deriving from the fact that the choice of format is a complex decision made by marketing, production and design staff. The question of consistency in design, for example, often arises when a book is licensed from a hardback publisher for direct transfer to paper-back production. If the new title is set in a typeface which differs from books by the same author, already in paperback, a decision must be made whether the paperback edition should be re-set. In such a case, the unit cost of the book, based on the size of the print-run, determines whether re-setting is economic.

Film-setting has inevitably altered the act of composing and the relationship between publisher and printer. The range of typefaces available for use in texts has been reduced considerably. If a wealth of reform had taken place in Monotype, with classical and more modern typefaces becoming accessible to the paperback designer, a comparable concern by Monophoto has yet to be shown. However, in film composition, the restriction in text typefaces has been compensated for by the display ranges suitable for cover designs. The disappearance of physical spacing, guaranteed in metal founts, led at first to erratic accidents in composition. Gradually books were designed which showed that this was not the result of something inherent in the technique. The *Complete Shakespeare*, published in 1969 jointly by Penguin Books Inc. and Allen Lane The Penguin Press, was the first Shakespeare edition to be filmset. Although when the American subsidiary had been re-established in 1950 under Harry Paroissien in Baltimore it was mainly for distribution of books manufactured in Harmondsworth, slowly it returned to originating and producing its own books. By 1967 the thirty-eight-volume Pelican Shakespeare had been published from Baltimore under the general editorship of Professor Alfred Harbage [c53]. From the beginning of 1968 a complete hardback Shakespeare was planned, composed in Monophoto Ehrhardt by the Westerham Press, who, like W. S. Cowell and Adprint in the case of King Penguins, had established a good reputation for high-quality 'craft' printing [c54]. A detailed account of its design by Hans Schmoller, and of its composition and printing, accompanied its publication on the anniversary of Shakespeare's birthday, 23 April 1969.

Not only prestige volumes were treated in this way. For example there was the attention paid to the Parallel Texts series, in which foreign-language prose was presented with its translation on the opposite page. One of the most exacting tasks was designing the typography of the Reference series, for example the *Dictionary of Decorative Arts* by Hugh Honour and John Fleming, a volume of 896 pages and with approximately 3,000 entries, of 1979.

PUFFIN'S PROGRESS

From 1960 to 1979, under their editorial director, Kaye Webb, Puffin had broadened its safe but reputable approach. The notion of a 'Puffin Land' – the idea that all children's tastes would be provided for – was encouraged by the list. The Puffin Club, reaching 47,000 members at its height, started in spring 1967 holding meetings with authors for children, arranging games and competitions, and organizing Saturday events for children who might otherwise be resistant to reading. It also provided a direct-mail service for children's purchases. *I Like This Poem*, a poetry collection made by children for other children, is characteristic of Kaye Webb's approach. So also was the extension to adventure and humour and the publishing of more contemporary writers, from Meindert De Jong to Roald Dahl. At the same time an attachment

to the standard titles of children's literature continued. This would lead eventually to the separate series, Puffin Classics, established in 1982.

As the range of Puffin extended, so the illustrations diversified. For children's own favourites there was an additional need for fantasy, the absurd, the exaggerated and the veristic. This could range from the hidden and detailed fantasy of *The Secret Garden* to the humour of *Stig of the Dump*, the popular space-travel illustrations in the sixties, nostalgic evocations of Victorian life, the lively characters of *The Family from One End Street* or the recent Fighting Fantasies (Figure 10).

A revival in the publication of Puffin Picture Books occurred in the late seventies, following the interest in the Russian illustrator Bilibin, the Swedish illustrator Carl Larsson

10. Gothic horror, provided here by Russ Nicholson for The Citadel of Chaos *in 1983, proved suitable for Fighting Fantasy Gamebooks.*

40 *A hunchbacked, mis-shapen creature with rotten teeth, ragged hair and tattered clothes stands in front of you.*

and Jugendstil book designs during the earlier part of the decade. In a review in 1976 this comment on the tremendous revival of children's publishing was made:

This renaissance exists even though children's books are at a higher level than they have ever been. Printing techniques have been refined to a point where almost any image can be reproduced. Methods are available to duplicate practically any quality of line or colour which the artist can conceive. Many of the mechanical limitations of the past, which so often dictated the style of the art, are non-existent. (Illustrators of Children's Books 1967–76, ed. Lee K. Natti et al., Horn Books. Boston, Mass., 1978, p.2)

THE 1970S: CONCEPTUAL GRAPHICS AND STYLISTIC REVIVALS IN DESIGN

After almost a year without a Fiction Art Editor, Penguin appointed David Pelham as Alan Aldridge's replacement in May 1968. His background had been in magazine design and reflected the professionalization of the graphic design industry which had occurred gradually during that decade in Britain. On leaving a General Graphics course at St Martin's School of Art, London, a course incorporating illustration and design, Pelham's first job in 1958 had been with *Ambassador* magazine. He then became art editor at Studio International before moving to *Harper's Bazaar* as their art director. The role of art direction well practised, Pelham saw the post at Penguin as a good opportunity to apply his approach to book design. Increasingly a large percentage of the cover artwork would be provided by outside design groups and illustrators, and to handle the work of commissioning within the Art Department there were seven in-house designers by 1980. Pelham's appointment took account of his knowledge of the British design world and his experience in delegating and coordinating design.

On his arrival Pelham's immediate concern was to establish coherence, a task made easier by lack of constraints:

Design was everything and commercial requirements were nothing. It was design very much for the sake of design and not design doing a hard job. (David Pelham in an interview, Designer magazine, December 1979)

Pelham introduced a grid which allowed maximum space within which the illustrators or designers could work. A border defined where the colophon should appear and also provided a guide for matching production size to prevent designs from being cropped at the printing stage. Pelham also organized the blurb space to be consistent between titles. Comparing his function with that of a telephone operator or a go-between, Pelham would read the book or be briefed on it by the editors, then he would select a suitable illustrator or designer, and in turn brief them verbally. On average 2.5 covers were conceived per day, with up to thirty covers at various stages of progress at one time. In 1969 *The Times* commented:

Penguin has no need of the blockbuster. It sells 27 million books a year, 22 million of which come from its backlist. (Julian Critchley: 'Hopes of Greater Rewards in the World of Publishing' 20 November 1969)

At a time when the backlist still seemed to be unchallenged, Penguin shared the complacency of *The Times*. The Fiction Art Department's prime function was to redesign existing titles with the intention of providing a cover which would last several printings, thereby paying its way.

Many of the designs which appeared after 1968 can be considered continuations or extensions of styles established in Aldridge's period. During that time, the place of commercial illustration had been asserted and fees fought for to make them comparable with those in photography and design. Pelham continued the experimental commissions of young or unknown designers, who contributed up to a quarter of the covers. For Science Fiction the tradition of black and purple covers was maintained, and illustrations provided by David Pelham or Philip Castle continued to be highly worked fantasies. Still-lifes for Crime Fiction, graphic puns and models, including those by Peter Fluck and Roger Law, were further signs of continuity [c55, c56 and c57].

The designs grew more confident and professional, a fact acknowledged by frequent awards, and Pelham used designers from many practices who were also award-winners for their non-Penguin work. On his own admission Pelham had 'always been wooed by a bit of polish'. With the assertion of a designer's identity coming from the whole cover, the identity of Penguin was to be found in a certain design quality rather than in the publisher's name [c58].

For fiction titles identity by author was encouraged. The Evelyn Waugh series designed by Peter Bentley provides an example of the use of period evocation in which the typography, the borders and the matt surface of the finish, as well as the illustrations, combine to form an Art-Deco revival. These and other covers in which pastiche was used proved highly effective; they also signified an altered attitude towards Modernism, which was finding expression in design and architecture at the time. The earlier Pop Art covers of Aldridge and Willock had referred to Art Nouveau lettering, and their impact was still intended to be new and different, whereas the period treatment which began in the early 1970s signified an increasing nostalgia and historicism in design [c60, c61 and c62].

Certain titles and authors, Waugh, Simenon, Colette and Scott Fitzgerald, for example, were given this identity. More serious fiction in the Modern Classics and English Library remained in the Facetti formula. Likewise Swiss-style typography was considered suitable for the Plays, in which a change in colour denoted a different group of playwrights [c59].

In the late sixties, Penguin Education, a series which developed into an independent imprint with its own editorial staff, was set up. It continued policies characteristic of its parent company, issuing many new series and even Penguin Education Specials on subjects of immediate significance. This separation of academic publishing reflected the growth in tertiary education in the late sixties and a wider move by Penguin into all levels of educational publishing. Most of all, Penguin Education's list acknowledged the growth in sociology, psychology and political science texts, and the writing of the New Left arising in the aftermath of May 1968.

At first the covers were conceived by the Penguin Education design staff. Later the series moved into primary and secondary education titles, and the complete list was given a house-style by an outside design group, Omnific. Designed and art directed by Derek Birdsall and Omnific, its identity was established by the predominance of black and white covers, which stressed the key words of the titles in bold typography on the front covers and on the spines. Sometimes a graphic symbol was found to characterize the theme of the book; in other cases a graphic pun on the title was made [c63]. A new colophon, designed by Derek Birdsall, served to identify the series. Parallels to this conceptual approach to graphic design can be found in contemporary packaging and so-called creative advertising, in which the importance of the copyline and play on words, and the significance of the depicted object, offered an alternative to conventional illustration and the decorative approach of Pop Art.

For the Pelican Marx Library, David Pelham commissioned David King to establish a series identity. King had worked on the *Sunday Times Supplement* as Art Editor from 1965 to 1975 and had developed a way of working which used titling as a constructive element in the design. He favoured using bold titling in capitals and tightly cropped photographs, and underlining sections of text by blocks of colour. This approach had established an important style of layout for photographic essays. When it came to the Marx titles King applied a similar approach [c64]. Appropriately he also used primary colours and tinted photographs of Karl Marx, a manner of working informed by the Soviet designer Alexander Rodchenko, whose posters and book designs had been an early example of art applied to mass-production.[4]

These last examples of Penguin book covers show how the scope of graphic design had broadened and developed during the sixties. It was no longer simply a choice between traditional or Swiss-style typography. Instead, designs revealed that the range available was from different kinds of illustration, photography, montage and conceptual approaches. To be 'modern' could mean adopting a functionalist approach, a standardized series with a house-style titling as the Facetti formula provided. On the other hand it could also mean the use of period pastiche and a stylistic evocation, with nostalgic typography and

4. Soviet design was an important influence on British design during the 1970s. For the work of Alexander Rodchenko and others, see Christina Lodder: *Russian Constructivism from Fine Art into Design*, Yale University Press, 1983.

layout matching period revivals in other forms of design and architecture.

In July 1970 Sir Allen Lane died. Just prior to his death, in articles written to commemorate his being made Companion of Honour, comparisons between Penguin and the BBC had been drawn and the suggestion made that Penguin Books could be seen as the publishing arm of the Beveridge Report. The following decade would call for a reassessment of policy for Penguin, as it would for the BBC. This would include adopting a more aggressive marketing policy, already anticipated in such cases as Richard Gordon's Doctor series in 1961 and Len Deighton's *Funeral in Berlin* in 1966. These changes would be marked in editorial policy, but also, in turn, in the expectations of book cover design from publisher, bookseller and public.

Concerned about the future of Penguin in the event of his death, Allen Lane had opened negotiations with a number of companies, including Longman, in the late sixties, and it was as Pearson Longman Ltd that the holding company bought Penguin Books for £15 million in 1970. Following what he had called the Godwin 'revolutionary' attempt, the policy which had become familiar as the Penguin identity was re-asserted in the last two years of Lane's control and turned out to be unaltered by corporate ownership. Under successive Chief Executives, Christopher Dolley, Peter Calvocoressi and Jim Rose, the general trend in the pattern of publishing was towards continuity. Economic difficulties beset Penguin, as they did all other publishers and manufacturers, during the recession of 1973–4. The first of these years saw an increase in production costs of 15 per cent, the second a continued rise to 20 per cent. Previously a crisis had been met by increasing the range of the lists. However, this response was ruled out by the rising costs of loans and the amount of money already in books and stocks. Instead, amidst industrial action, Peter Calvocoressi reluctantly reduced the staff by 10 per cent in 1975, some authors' contracts were cancelled and the annual sum of books to be published reduced from 780 to 520 in that year and finally to 450 by 1977. A contributory factor to Penguin's difficulties occurred in 1974, when three major hardback publishers reclaimed the paperback rights of authors whose works were symbolic of the calibre of the Penguin Fiction backlist. Faced with the growth and diversification of the paperback market and the fact that hardback sales were not growing, publishers became keen to secure books for paperback companies with which they themselves were directly associated. Subsequently the names of Hemingway, Huxley, Joyce, Maugham, Murdoch, Steinbeck and Woolf disappeared from Penguin shelves. As licences for authors' work came up for renewal, so publishers reverted to a new imprint of their own, called Triad, which was distributed by Granada, or in Heinemann's case to Pan, one third of whose shares they owned. The underlying motive was the desire of these hardback publishers for a part of the paperback market, as opposed to higher paperback royalties. At the same time the rapid expansion of Penguin Education was proving economically unviable, and its demise as a separate division was followed by the incorporation of some of the titles in the Pelican, and later Penguin, list.

Clearly the brief of providing 'good literature for the intelligent layman' had been superseded by the tremendous growth in readership of paperbacks in post-war Britain. Penguin's position was affected by the development of special-interest publishers in the early and mid-seventies, aimed at minority markets, whether literary fiction as in the case of Picador and Virago, or academic publishing with New Left Books, the Oxford University Press paperback wing, the Writers' and Readers' Press and Paladin. In such cases the design solution was very often guided by Penguin's earlier policies, especially in the case of Virago, where Facetti's formula of matching paintings to titles was used. At the same time Penguin had to look towards the growth in the 'blockbuster' approach to paperbacks made by mass-market publishers. The 'blockbusters' consist of books chosen for the 'front' list.[5] With enormous cash advances to the author, certain titles are bought for mass-promotion, with simultaneous display in major trade outlets, whether in railway bookstalls, newsagents or the traditional bookshops. As part of

5. See: 'Blockbuster Complex', three articles in the *New Yorker*, 29 September, 6 and 13 October 1980.

the promotion, authors are sent on nationwide tours, while interviews are arranged for television and radio coverage.

On his appointment as Chief Executive at Penguin in 1978, Peter Mayer was sensitive to these seemingly contradictory trends in the paperback field, but his essential task was to make Penguin competitive again. His background was in American publishing, where he had been Editor-in-Chief then Publisher at Avon Books, then President and Publisher at Pocket Books, the paperback imprint of Simon and Schuster in the United States. He contended that if Penguin's backlist was to be maintained, it was essential to guarantee a group of lead titles which would strengthen the front list. The first of these, M. M. Kaye's *The Far Pavilions*, had already been published by the hardback imprint Allen Lane before Mayer arrived [c67].

It was essential to publish new and exciting works that would become a future backlist. (Peter Mayer, June 1985)

Mayer felt that he needed to fight the hesitancy towards commercial attitudes within Penguin.

What was different about my approach was the way books were presented, priced and marketed. Larger and more varied formats were introduced for the paperback book. Some books could be aggressively packaged, priced higher and given more targeted marketing. (ibid.)

NEW SERIES: NEW DESIGNS

Cover design requirements are inevitably affected by mass-promotion. The need for paperback houses to compete for shelf-space, where books were now displayed by subject rather than by imprint, is a significant determinant. As much as 25 per cent of Penguins are sold through outlets other than bookshops, serviced by large wholesalers such as Bookwise and W. H. Smith Distributors. In order to secure this important part of the market, Penguin covers must satisfy these distributors, who review them monthly. They believe they can judge the kind of commercial solution that will make a book saleable. Resistance towards such demands on design has been voiced by several art directors:

Many paperback houses have put pressure on their art departments to produce so-called selling covers, dripping with gold-blocking, resulting in a marked drop in design standards, but they still end up on the remainder shelf looking like old tarts. (Mike Dempsey, former Art Director, Fontana Books, in *Design*, September 1980, p.9)

But unless the design fulfils their criteria in its appearance at this stage, the publisher risks losing the opportunity of such trade outlets altogether.

The film or TV tie-in is another important aspect in such promotion. An early case, the *Quatermass* scripts of 1959, simply saw the Penguin tripartite formula changed to suggest a television screen. By 1968, the Galsworthy novels benefited from five-colour reproduction, when scenes from the highly successful BBC television adaptation were used on the covers. This is now the pattern. The lifespan varies but it is often no longer than three months. A recent strategy has been to publish a larger, more expensive tie-in edition, to be sold concurrently with the existing one. A recent example was Evelyn Waugh's *Brideshead Revisited* in 1984.

Two examples of changes in the Fiction list are characteristic of design being used more actively in marketing titles. Graham Greene's titles had become established with Paul Hogarth's illustrations, originally commissioned by David Pelham. After 1980 the scale of the titling was increased and a new illustration commissioned from Paul Hogarth to be reproduced in colour. A small amount of copy was also incorporated on the front cover. Another example was the C. S. Forester series. Here a more complete revision occurred – instead of reproducing paintings from the National Maritime Museum, an illustration intended to have a wider appeal was used. However, in this case the new formula did not increase sales [c65 to c68].

Some titles are now treated individually to the extent that they lose the Penguin identity. If a book is considered to require such treatment, it may be packaged so extensively that the colophon is lost amidst a struggle of blurb, title and illustration. Even works which had previously been the preserve of literary fiction could be given mass-market treatment. The alternative, it is considered, is to risk underselling the title for the sake of maintaining identity. At the beginning of this return to competitive packaging at Penguin, the Sales

Department suggested that not only should the orange spine be dropped, but also the colophon. They considered that these had become impediments to distributing books in certain outlets. Mayer refused to lose the colophon, arguing that in time Penguin would once again become associated, in the minds of the bookseller, with this broader range of publishing. However, while a number of Penguin's publications are given this individual treatment, new series have been launched since 1978 and others revised which continue the traditional approach. In such series a house-style is an essential editorial and design ingredient.

Following the 1960s, in which there was a proliferation of design groups and the place of art direction had been acknowledged in Britain, illustration experienced a considerable revival. This coincided with a move away from photographic and montage concepts, and the loss of certain faith in Modernism as the single set of principles suitable for all book design. The influence of illustrators was acknowledged by the rise of galleries dealing specifically in their work, while a code of practice was formulated, amongst other things, by the Association of Illustrators in 1973. Consequently freelance illustrators have become a major source for covers, their work arriving in the Art Department in diverse media and sizes, to be integrated by the in-house designers into covers, complete with title, author, blurb, ISBN number and bar-code for retailing. After eleven years as Penguin's Art Director, David Pelham left to work as a freelance designer before joining Pentagram. He was succeeded in 1980 by Cherriwyn Magill, who was returning to Penguin after a period with Macmillan.

For the revised design of the Penguin Modern Classics the grey panel and fully bled reproduction was changed by Cherriwyn Magill to an orange and white design, retaining the reproduction. According to the title, the Modern Classics are either in traditional format or in the larger 'B' format. In certain titles, a commissioned illustration is used [c69]. Following changing tastes in the wider art and design environment, Victorian paintings and figurative works of the interwar years occur more frequently. The picture editor selects works which 'illustrate' the character of the novel, rather than making a formal parallel, which had been Facetti's policy when he introduced the idea [c74].

Outside design groups have been commissioned to design house-styles for series, which, once established, are then varied by individual commissions for each title, or otherwise designed in the Art and Design Departments. This was the case for the Reference series, re-cast in 1982. The black and red covers of the past gave way to a basically white design. Colour-coded by a small stripe on the spine, they have a commissioned illustration inserted in a panel on the front and grey titling designed by Ken Carroll and Mike Dempsey [c77].

The present Art Director, Steve Kent, has reinforced this policy, which confirms Penguin's position as an important patron of new illustrators. Covers using montage or typographical arrangements are often designed within the firm. This is the case, for example, when Pelicans from the backlist are re-cast, and torn-paper styles, much larger typography and magazine techniques are adopted. There are parallels between the eighties and the mid-sixties; then, as now, a nexus of graphic design, fashion and music made a strong impact. As in the past, opinion about these changes is divided. The Art Director is faced with a much broader and more catholic brief, which makes his position both more complex and more stimulating.

The new King Penguin series, started in 1981, concentrated on contemporary fiction. To match the more speculative end of publishing, innovative covers are commissioned. At first these were incorporated into Carroll and Dempsey's house-style – a white spine, with a grey title panel appearing on the spine and front cover [c70 and c72]. A third series, with a house-style by the design group Nicholas Thirkell and Partners, is the Lives and Letters. Steve Kent has commissioned a series of portraits by Lawrence Mynott for the covers, which are treated in a manner suited to the period of writing [c76]. Begun in 1984 in large format, they consist of literary biographies, autobiographies and collected writings. Some titles, as is also the case in the Travel Library, are from Penguin's backlist, retrieved and given a new prominence; others are new.

If a characteristic common to all these series can be found, it is in the preference for serifed letter forms, centred titling and illustrations contained within borders. The front and back cover as well as the spine all work towards the unity of design.

After twenty-two years, the Classics series has been given a new format to coincide with a change in the concept of the series. The English and American Libraries, many twentieth-century works of literature and a number of anthologies have been brought into the Classics list, supplementing the regular ancient and modern language translations. The cover design, by Kent, demonstrates the changed response to typography and decoration in contemporary design. While the formula of reproducing a sculpture or painting, or a detail of an object which reflects the book's theme, is retained, the reproduction is sometimes inset, headed by centred titling. In the proportions applied, the choice of Sabon typeface and the general tone of the covers, comparisons can be made with Jan Tschichold's covers for the 1947 series [c79]. However, technically they originate in very different ways, and the decision to use colour

reproduction and apply certain letter-spacing is now unimpeded by limitations in craft skills or technology.

If a conclusion can be drawn on the nature of changes in typography and cover artwork in Penguin's history, it would refer to the context of paperback market requirements. Questions related to the co-production of books are normally central ones for typographic designers, but the distinction between paperback and cloth as regards the insides of books has in large measure been broken down by technological developments. Similarly, the trend of cover artwork and the decisions made in art direction will be partly in response to the changing range of available styles of design and illustration, but will increasingly take into account the requirements of publishing with the film and computer media. Underlying such developments, none the less, is the debate about the quality of the interior and exterior design of books. The debate will continue to raise questions concerning principles of typographic design and the appropriateness of form, as it has done over the last fifty years of Penguin Books.

LIST OF COLOUR ILLUSTRATIONS

Plate	Author / Book title	Designer (D) Illustrator (I) Photographer (P)	Size (st = 'A' format, 181 × 111 mm)	Date
C1	The first ten	D: Edward Young	st	1935
C2	Claude Houghton: Hudson Rejoins the Herd	D: Hans (Giovanni) Mardersteig	178 × 102 mm	1947
C3	Bernard Shaw: The Intelligent Woman's Guide to Socialism, Capitalism, Sovietism & Fascism	D: Edward Young	st	1937
C4	Edgar Mowrer: Germany Puts the Clock Back	D: Edward Young	st	1937
C5	Izaak Walton: The Compleat Angler	D: Edward Young I: Gertrude Hermes	st	1939
C6	Melville: Typee	D: Edward Young I: Robert Gibbings	st	1938
C7	Redouté, edited by Elizabeth Senior: A Book of Roses	D: John Overton	187 × 124 mm	1939
C8	Kenneth Rowntree and Gwyn Jones: A Prospect of Wales	D: Jan Tschichold Technical Editor: R. B. Fishenden	187 × 124 mm	1948
C9	Alfred Fairbank: A Book of Scripts	D: Jan Tschichold Technical Editor: R. B. Fishenden	187 × 124 mm	1949
C10	Kathleen Hale: Orlando's Evening Out	D and I: Kathleen Hale	181 × 222 mm	1941
C11	Chiang Yee: Lo Cheng	D and I: Chiang Yee	181 × 222 mm	1942
C12	Margaret and Alexander Potter: A History of the Countryside	D and I: Margaret and Alexander Potter	178 × 222 mm	1944
C13	Myfanwy Evans: Frances Hodgkins	D: Jan Tschichold	178 × 222 mm	1948
C14	Bertil Hultén: Building Modern Sweden	D: Erik Frederiksen P: C. G. Rosenberg	178 × 222 mm	1951

Plate	Author / Book title	Designer (D) Illustrator (I) Photographer (P)	Size (st = 'A' format, 181 × 111 mm)	Date
C15	Editor John Lehmann: *The Penguin New Writing No. 1*	Unknown	st	1940
C16	Editor John Lehmann: *The Penguin New Writing No. 31*	I: John Minton	181 × 121 mm	1947
C17	Back cover of R. A. Saville-Sneath: *Aircraft Recognition* showing advertisement	Unknown	st	1941
C18	Homer: *The Odyssey*	D: Jan Tschichold Device by William Grimmond	st	1948
C19	Evelyn Waugh: *Vile Bodies*	D: Jan Tschichold P: Madame Yevonde	st	1948
C20	Bernard Shaw: *Saint Joan*	D: Hans Schmoller Film title by: Saul Bass P: top: Malcolm Arbuthnot; bottom: John Jay	st	1957
C21	Lytton Strachey: *Eminent Victorians*	D: Hans Schmoller	st	1951
C22	William Faulkner: *The Wild Palms*	D: Hans Schmoller Device by Berthold Wolpe	st	1961
C23	Patience Gray and Primrose Boyd: *Plats du Jour*	D: Hans Schmoller I: David Gentleman	st	1957
C24	Editor N. Pevsner: *The Buildings of England Wiltshire*	D: Hans Schmoller	st	1963
C25	Pelican History of Art pamphlet	D: Hans Schmoller Colophon by Berthold Wolpe	248 × 178 mm	1953
C26	Basil Maine: *Edward VIII – Duke of Windsor* Hutchinson Pocket Library No. 18	Unknown	181 × 108 mm	c.1940
C27	John Buchan: *Mr Standfast*	D: Hans Schmoller I: Stephen Russ	st	1956
C28	Advertisement card for Andrew Rothstein: *A History of the U.S.S.R.*	D: Hans Schmoller	496 × 292 mm	1950
C29	Walt Whitman: *Leaves of Grass*	D: Lucian Bernhard I: Rafaello Busoni	165 × 114 mm	1943
C30	Carson McCullers: *The Heart is a Lonely Hunter*	D: Robert Jonas	st	1946

Plate	Author / Book title	Designer (D) Illustrator (I) Photographer (P)	Size (st = 'A' format, 181 × 111 mm)	Date
c31	Virginia Woolf: Orlando	D: George Salter	st	1946
c32	Ruth Benedict: Patterns of Culture	D: Robert Jonas	st	1946
c33	Paul Brickhill: The Great Escape	D: Abram Games and Hans Schmoller	st	1957
c34	Editor A. Alvarez: The New Poetry	D: Hans Schmoller I: Stephen Russ	st	1962
c35	Penguin Music Scores 6 Schubert: Symphony No. 8	D: Hans Schmoller and Elizabeth Friedländer	127 × 197 mm	1950
c36	Editor A. Alvarez: The New Poetry	D: Germano Facetti Reproduction of Jackson Pollock: Convergence, Albright-Knox Gallery, Buffalo, New York	st	1966
c37	Len Deighton: London Dossier	D: Len Deighton	st	1967
c38	Ed McBain: Killer's Wedge	D: Romek Marber and Alan Spain P: Don Hunstein	st	1964
c39	G. K. Chesterton: The Innocence of Father Brown	D: Romek Marber	st	1962
c40	Penguin Bookshop interior designed by Germano Facetti			1965
c41	Penguin Modern Poets 8: Edwin Brock, Geoffrey Hill, Stevie Smith	D: Alan Spain	st	1966
c42	Bertrand Russell: Has Man a Future?	D: Richard Hollis	st	1962
c43	John Braine: Room at the Top	D: Hans Schmoller Photograph of Laurence Harvey as Joe Lampton in the Romulus film, 1959	st	1959
c44	Alan Sillitoe: Saturday Night and Sunday Morning Pan Books	D: Hans Helweg	178 × 108 mm	1960
c45	Bertolt Brecht: Threepenny Novel	D: Germano Facetti Reproduction of George Grosz: The Robbers, George Grosz Estate, Princeton, New Jersey	st	1965

Plate	Author/Book title	Designer (D) Illustrator (I) Photographer (P)	Size (st = 'A' format, 181 × 111 mm)	Date
c46	Jean-Paul Sartre: The Age of Reason	D: Germano Facetti Reproduction of Pablo Picasso: Guernica, Copyright DACS 1985	st	1981 reprint
c47	Edna O'Brien: Girls in their Married Bliss	D: Alan Aldridge	st	1967
c48	Colin Watson: Hopjoy Was Here	D: Alan Aldridge and Brian Haynes P: Dennis Rolfe	st	1966
c49	Keith Waterhouse: Jubb	D: Alan Aldridge P: Richard Heimann	st	1966
c50	Alfred Bester: Tiger! Tiger!	D: Alan Aldridge	st	1967
c51	Laurence Sickman and Alexander Soper: The Art and Architecture of China The Pelican History of Art	D: Gerald Cinamon Photograph: Detail of a wall- painting of AD 706 in the tomb of Princess Yung T'ai, Shensi Province	210 × 148 mm	1971
c52	Henri Frankfort: The Art and Architecture of the Ancient Orient The Pelican History of Art	D: Gerald Cinamon Photograph: Audience Hall of Darius and Xerxes, Persepolis. Copyright Trustees of the British Museum	210 × 148 mm	1979
c53	Twelfth Night The Pelican Shakespeare Editor Charles Prouty Penguin Books Inc.	D: Fritz Kredel	st	1972
c54	Leaflet for the Complete Pelican Shakespeare	D: Hans Schmoller	280 × 216 mm	1969
c55	Colette: Chéri and The Last of Chéri	D: David Pelham P: Copyright H. Roger Viollet and Société des Amis de Colette	198 × 129 mm	1973
c56	Robert Newill: Infertile Marriage	D: David Pelham and Mel Calman	st	1974
c57	Graham Cleverley: Managers and Magic	D: David Pelham and Peter Fluck	st	1973
c58	D. H. Lawrence: Sea and Sardinia	D: David Pelham and Harri Peccinotti	st	1974
c59	New English Dramatists 7 Arnold Wesker, David Rudkin, Giles Cooper	D: Henning Boehlke	st	1971

Plate	Author / Book title	Designer (D) Illustrator (I) Photographer (P)	Size (st = 'A' format, 181 × 111 mm)	Date
c60	Evelyn Waugh: *The Ordeal of Gilbert Pinfold*	D: Peter Bentley	st	1972
c61	Raymond Chandler: *Playback*	D: James Tormey Photographs: courtesy 20th Century-Fox, Warner Brothers and RKO Pictures	st	1971
c62	W. Somerset Maugham: *The Moon and Sixpence* *Cakes and Ale* *The Narrow Corner*	D: Derek Birdsall P: Harri Peccinotti	st	1971
c63	*The Paint House:* *Words from an East End Gang*	D: Omnific / Martin Causer	st	1972
c64	Karl Marx: *The First International and After*	D: David King	198 × 129 mm	1974
c65	C. S. Forester: *The Commodore*	D: David Pelham Photograph: Reproduction of 'Ships of the East India Company', N. Pocock (1741–1821), National Maritime Museum	st	1975
c66	C. S. Forester: *The Commodore*	I: Kenneth Wynn	st	1980
c67	M. M. Kaye: *The Far Pavilions*	I: Peter Goodfellow	198 × 129 mm	1979
c68	Graham Greene: *A Burnt-Out Case*	D: David Pelham I: Paul Hogarth	st	1983
c69	Franz Kafka: *The Castle*	D: Steve Kent I: Liz Pyle	st	1984
c70	Milan Kundera: *The Farewell Party*	D: Ken Carroll and Mike Dempsey I: Andrzej Klimowski	198 × 129 mm	1984
c71	Ian Watt: *The Rise of the Novel*	D: Cherriwyn Magill I: Tom Woodruff	198 × 129 mm	1983
c72	John Kennedy Toole: *A Confederacy of Dunces*	D: Ken Carroll and Mike Dempsey I: Ed Lindlof	198 × 129 mm	1981
c73	Homer: *The Odyssey*	D: Germano Facetti Photograph of *Odysseus*, a bronze relief, courtesy of the Department of Antiquities, Berlin	st	1983
c74	Henry James: *The Portrait of a Lady*	D: Steve Kent Reproduction of Edmund C. Tarbell: *Reverie*, courtesy of Boston Museum of Fine Arts	st	1984

Plate	Author / Book title	Designer (D) Illustrator (I) Photographer (P)	Size (st = 'A' format, 181 × 111 mm)	Date
c75	Mikhail Sholokhov: *Harvest on the Don*	D: Cherriwyn Magill Reproduction of Kasimir Malevich: *Taking in the Rye*, courtesy of the Stedelijk Museum, Amsterdam	198 × 129 mm	1984
c76	Osbert Sitwell: *Left Hand, Right Hand!*	D: Nicholas Thirkell & Partners I: Lawrence Mynott	210 × 198 mm	1984
c77	Rosalind Ferguson: *The Penguin Dictionary of Proverbs*	D: Mike Dempsey and Ken Carroll I: Bob Haberfield	198 × 129 mm	1984
c78	Helge Rubinstein: *The Chocolate Book*	D: Cherriwyn Magill P: Tessa Traeger	198 × 129 mm	1982
c79	Mary Shelley: *Frankenstein*	D: Steve Kent Reproduction of Joseph Wright: *A Hermit Studying Anatomy*, courtesy of Derby Museum and Art Gallery	st	1985
c80	The Penguin Poetry Library: *Pope*	D: Steve Kent Reproduction of *Portrait of Pope* (attributed to Jonathan Richardson), courtesy of National Portrait Gallery, London	st	1985
c81	A Puffin Quartet of Poets E. Farjeon, J. Reeves, I. Serraillier and E. V. Rieu	D: Diana Bloomfield	198 × 129 mm	1984
c82	Richard Adams: *Watership Down*	I: Pauline Baynes	st	1983
c83	Paul Theroux: *London Snow*	I: John Lawrence	198 × 129 mm	1982
c84	E. Nesbit: *The Phoenix and the Carpet*	I: H. R. Millar	st	1984

ACKNOWLEDGEMENTS

Items in the exhibition have been kindly loaned by the following people and institutions, many of whom have given invaluable advice and information:

Alan Aldridge
Colin Aldridge
H. Arnold
Ian Ballantine
H. L. Beales
R. C. Boar
Henning Boehlke
Patrick Bossert
Andrea Breese
L. A. Burman
Gerald Cinamon
Margaret Clark
B. B. Clifford
J. M. Cohen
Fergus Corcoran
Andrew Dalby
Robert Davies
John Elsley
Lady Elwyn-Jones
Margaret M. Enoch
Germano Facetti
Stuart Flanagan
Michael Foxwell
Eunice Frost
Eric Gadd
Milton Glaser
Arnold Greenwood
S. Gunasena
Ralph Gustafson
R. Gutfreund
Cicely Hammond
Basil Harley

Malcolm Hawdon
Tim Hawkins
Walter Hayes
David Hedges
John Hitchin
Paul Hogarth
Robert Hollingsworth
J. C. Homan
David Howlett
John Hudson
Grace Hunt
Mary G. Jones
Jack Kendle
Baron Bernd von Keyserlingk
David King
Peter Lord
Dr Duncan McGarva
Heather Mansell
Romek Marber
John Mercer
John Miles
W. R. Mitchell
Professor J. E. Morpurgo
Simon Newton
G. R. Nicholls
Eric Norris
Iain C. Orr
John Overton
David Pelham
Peter Perchard
Dieter Pevsner
Alick and Margaret Potter

Jack Pritchard
William Radice
Glyn Russ
Douglas Rust
Pat Schleger
Hans and Tatyana Schmoller
Piet Schreuders
Geoffrey Smith
Alan Spain
Meaburn Staniland
Richard Storey
David Sutherland
Teresa Topolski
P. F. Tunstill
Boris Uvarov
Elliott Viney
A. F. Wallis
Nora Weaver
Kaye Webb
Harry Willock
Edward Young

Richard Clay plc
Collet's Penguin Bookshop
W. S. Cowell Ltd
Hazell, Watson & Viney Ltd
High Commission of India
Paul Popper Ltd
Publisher's Association
University Library, Bristol
University
University of Newcastle-upon-Tyne

For permission to reproduce copyright material in the exhibition and in this book we wish to thank:

Albright-Knox Gallery, Buffalo,
    New York
Allen & Unwin Ltd
Ian Ballantine
BBC Hulton Picture Library
Nicolas Bentley
Bookseller
Boston Museum of Fine Arts
Jonathan Cape Ltd
Chatto & Windus Ltd
DACS
Daily Express
Daily Mail

Department of Antiquities, Berlin
Derby Museum and Art Gallery
Economist
Estate of the late Sonia Brownell
    Orwell and Martin Secker &
    Warburg Ltd
Financial Times
Fay Godwin
George Grosz Estate, Princeton,
    New Jersey
Guardian
Guildhall Library
Tom Harrisson Mass-Observation
    Archive

Frank Herrmann
Michael Heath
Professor Richard Hoggart
Imperial War Museum
The late Richard Lane
London Zoo
Sir Robert Lusty
Heather Mansell
Robert Maynard
Professor J. E. Morpurgo
National Maritime Museum
National Portrait Gallery
New Statesman

ACKNOWLEDGEMENTS

Pan Books Ltd
Publisher's Weekly
Punch
Société des amis de Colette
Sprod

Stedelijk Museum, Amsterdam
The Times Newspapers Ltd
The Times Educational Supplement
The Times Literary Supplement
Topham Picture Library

Transworld Publishing Ltd
Trustees of the British Museum
20th Century-Fox, Warner
   Brothers and RKO Pictures
H. Roger Viollet

For help with the exhibition and in the preparation of this book, the authors also particularly wish to thank:

Graham Beattie
Françoise Berserick
Caroline Bugler
Marcia Burch
John Burrows
Noel Carrington
Hannah Cinamon
Kate Cinamon
Sara Cinamon
Charles Clark
John Curtis
David Duguid
Don Flowerdew
Peter Fluck
Trevor Glover
Evelyne Green
Ellen Grout
Susan Hagan
Richard Hildersley
Catherine Holmes
J. A. Holmes
Michael Holroyd

Rosemary Ind
Thomas Joy
Steve Kent
Peter Kite
Roger Law
Ruari McLean
Bill McMullan
Cherriwyn Magill
Sylvia Mogg
Arthur Mould
Robin Myers
Judy Nairn
H. F. Paroissien
Neil Philip
Fred Price
John Rolfe
E. J. B. Rose
Beth Ross
Peter Rozycki
Gillian Schwab
Doreen Scott
John Seaton
J. J. Strating

H. H. Summers
David and Christine Teale
Feliks Topolski
Eric Tripp
Jonathan Yglesias

FGS Print Services Ltd (Francis
   Gregory)
National Book League (Margaret
   Payne)
National Portrait Gallery (Roger
   Sheppard)
Oxford Polytechnic (R. B.
   Woodings)
Penguin Collectors' Society
   (Richard Hazelhurst)
St Bride Printing Library (James
   Moseley)
W. H. Smith Ltd (T. W. Baker-
   Jones)
University of Reading (J. A.
   Edwards)

Fifty Penguin Years